WITHDRAWN

DANGER
MAN WORKING

W9-CGL-012

ALSO BY MICHAEL PERRY

BOOKS

AUDIO

MUSIC

DANGER
MAN WORKING

WRITING FROM THE HEART, THE GUT,
AND THE POISON IVY PATCH

MICHAEL PERRY

WISCONSIN HISTORICAL SOCIETY PRESS

Published by the Wisconsin Historical Society Press
Publishers since 1855

The Wisconsin Historical Society helps people connect to the past by collecting, preserving, and sharing stories. Founded in 1846, the Society is one of the nation's finest historical institutions.
Order books by phone toll free: (888) 999-1669
Order books online: shop.wisconsinhistory.org
Join the Wisconsin Historical Society: wisconsinhistory.org/membership

Printed in Canada
Cover design by TG Design
Typesetting by Ryan Scheife, Mayfly Design

21 20 19 18 17   1 2 3 4 5

Library of Congress Cataloging-in-Publication Data
Names: Perry, Michael, 1964– author.
Title: Danger, man working : writing from the heart, the gut, and the poison ivy patch / Michael Perry.
Other titles: Writing from the heart, the gut, and the poison ivy patch
Description: 1st edition. | Madison, WI : Wisconsin Historical Society Press, [2017] |
Identifiers: LCCN 2017018701 (print) | LCCN 2017027870 (e-book) | ISBN 9780870208416 (E-book) | ISBN 9780870208409 (pbk. : alk. paper)
Subjects: LCSH: Wisconsin—Social life and customs—Anecdotes. | Perry, Michael, 1964——Family. | United States—Social life and customs—Anecdotes. | Popular culture—United States.
Classification: LCC F581.6 (e-book) | LCC F581.6 .P47 2017 (print) | DDC 977.5—dc23
LC record available at https://lccn.loc.gov/2017018701

♾ The paper used in this publication meets the minimum requirements of the American National Standard for Information Sciences—Permanence of Paper for Printed Library Materials, ANSI Z39.48-1992.

To Miss Grant. Senior year in high school. I took her class for all the wrong reasons. Figured I was sneaking a low-effort credit. Rather than treat me like the adolescent know-it-all I was, she smiled and did her job, teaching me a skill I have used nearly every day for the past 30 years as a means of employment, of feeding my kids, and of utterly unanticipated adventure, joy, and fulfillment.

Miss Grant taught me how to type.

CREDITS

"Shock and Awe," "Mushing" (as "Dogsledding in Minnesota: Born to Run"), and "Running the River Righteous" originally appeared in *Backpacker Magazine.*

"Musky Hunting" and "Poison Ivy *Where?*" (as "Itchy and Scratchy") originally appeared in *Outside Magazine.*

"My Daughter's Father," "The Not-So Handyman" (as "Danger: Man Working"), "Tim McGraw: Real Good Bad Example" (as "Re-Born in the USA"), "New Year's Resolution: Meet Mills at the Widowmaker" (as "Resolution: I Will Hang with Pals"), "Health Secrets from the Morgue",* "Puking (as "Meet Ralph")," "Mike Is Sweaty" (as "Sweat, the Details"), "Mike Eats Beans" (as "Escape from Statins"), "That Ears Ringing Thing" (as "The Hellish Din in My Head"), "Teetotal" (as "Hey Doc, Should I Start Drinking?"), "Like Mother, Like Son," and "A Philosopher for the Rest of Us" (as "5 Timeless Life Tips") originally appeared in *Men's Health Magazine.*

"Greg Brown: Hallelujah Anyway" originally appeared in *No Depression* magazine.

"King Pleasure"** and "Letter to Lightnin' Hopkins" originally appeared in *The Oxford American.*

"Molly and the Heymakers" originally appeared in *Wisconsin Trails* magazine.

"The Power and the Glory" originally appeared in *Runner's World.*

"Sublimation: The Blind Boys of Alabama" originally appeared as liner notes in the album *I'll Find a Way.*

"Working" originally appeared in the Wisconsin Humanities Council newsletter.

Note: Some of these essays wound up recut and repurposed in book form; likewise, some have been refashioned from the books themselves.

---

*   Also included in *Best American Science and Nature Writing 2007.*

**   Also included in *The Oxford American Book of Great Music Writing.*

CONTENTS

INTRODUCTION

Every writer has advice for aspiring writers. Mine is predicated on formative years spent cleaning my father's calf pens: Just keep shoveling until you've got a pile so big, *someone* has to notice. The fact that I cast my life's work as slung manure simply proves that I recognize an apt metaphor when I accidentally stick it with a pitchfork.

I often wish I were purely artful. I am forever indebted to the true poets who led me to fall in love with words afresh and anew relatively late in life—after college, when I had a nursing degree and a good job, and figured I was on my way. The poets detoured me with words, immersed me in words, imbued me with the idea that I might want to *write* words.

I took the leap, and I have never regretted it. But perhaps because I made the leap late—after working on Dad's Wisconsin farm; as a Wyoming ranch hand; as a construction gofer; as a roller-skating Snoopy; on a mental health unit; for a surgeon; on a neurological rehabilitation unit; weekends on the ambulance—I was pretty clear-eyed about the likelihood that I could pay the rent with poems alone. And so I read everything I could about freelancing, and started shoveling.

So it goes until this day, and so it will always go unless I sell a million.

The pieces in this collection are drawn from the past fifteen years of shovel time. We (each piece and this book itself only came to be through the work of excellent, encouraging, and patient editors) divvied them up in sections, but the idea that there is thematic flow is superficially imposed. Basically what you have here is me going to work as the work is offered. There are essays on puke, sweat, and cholesterol. Articles with—and you'll recognize them when you read them—"service" sentences, in which the editor has instructed the writer to deliver some "actionable" information. I hope the inclusion of these more prosaic pieces speaks to the fundamental element of writing as work. It's lovely to weave a wicker chair, but sometimes the client (and proxy mortgage payer) wants a stackable straight-back. Pure art, nope. But even in these pieces, you try to pay attention to the rhythm of the prose, try to paint evocative scenes, try to sneak in a wink, a grin, a moment of compassion.

Some of the pieces are dated—in both reference (Jimmy Swaggart and Paris Hilton?) and style, and sometimes embarrassingly so. (In the department of Recurring Themes, it quickly becomes obvious that I am a self-absorbed hypochondriac forever resolving to do better nutritionally and fitness-wise but my follow-through is laughable.) There were times I wanted to cut or revise words or passages that grate on me now in ways they didn't when I wrote them (a few offhand lines about women and one about incarceration really reddened my face). But in most cases I've decided it's best to lay them out there the way they were in hopes that they stand as evidence to some improvement of thought and style on my part. That a knucklehead might evolve.

Then there are those pieces where I was turned loose, free to write as I pleased. These are my favorites. The ones that take me on flights reminiscent of how I felt in those early poetry days. When you are allowed to trade the shovel for wings, even as you stand there in your boots. Rereading those pieces, I was again filled with gratitude for this lifelong sidetrack.

And finally there are those stories—the very first piece in this collection chief among them—in which I realize once again that as a writer, I find my greatest privilege lies not in telling my story; it lies in being trusted to tell the story of another.

MEN AMONG MEN

SHOCK AND AWE

Yesterday, retired Army National Guard First Lieutenant Ed Salau slipped the scarred stump of his left leg into a $30,000 hydraulic-fitted carbon-fiber and titanium prosthesis and headed for the top of Mount Rainier.

He didn't make it.

But the end of the climb is not the end of the story. The story is how Salau—a trim man who still carries himself with the bearing of his 12 years as a Marine—stomped his way up to Camp Muir, well short of the summit but well above the clouds. How he went barefoot in the snow. Why—even knowing he would go no higher—he spent an afternoon flinging himself face-first into the slush, rehearsing self-arrest and getting kicked in the noggin for his efforts. And then there are all those terrific campfire tales only a one-legged man can tell—the one about the kid in Dunkin' Donuts, the one about the woman in the bar, and the one where he tells his teenage boy, "Son, I will plant my foot in your ass and leave it there!" The one about spotting the guy with the grenade launcher right about the time it fired.

There will be time for the stories. But right now it is late afternoon. The light is beginning to flatten across the Cowlitz Glacier. Several climbing groups are preparing for summit attempts, and there is a bustle of to and fro throughout the smattering of tents pitched in the Muir notch. Salau's group will strike out at 11 p.m., hoping to stand atop Rainier by morning. Earlier, the guides huddled, and then one of them—Art Rausch, who's summited Rainier

3

150 times—separated from the group to speak quietly with Salau. We've talked it over, said Rausch, and it's just not going to work.

Ed Salau understands why he is being left behind. Despite everything he has done since his last two-legged day on earth—skydiving, waterskiing, downhill skiing, running—he has learned, he says, that you are not going anywhere that one leg won't let you go. It is not about admitting defeat; rather it is about acknowledging reality. And there is strength in that.

But right here in the moment, he cannot lie. He is not happy. That is why he has taken himself away from the group to stare off at the foothills of eastern Washington, to watch them go orange as the day fades. He has walked away from the tents a good distance. His back is turned to the campsite. He holds himself ramrod straight between the crutches, and he wishes he were somewhere else.

He feels, he says, like the last kid picked.

Down among the tents, Captain Scott Smiley is trying to rest. He is propped against a backpack, awaiting supper. Smiley is a big man, broad-shouldered, with the reasonable musculature of a pre-steroidal tight end. His catalog-worthy features—bold but proportionate nose, wide cheekbones, and a solid outcropping of jaw—are nicely normalized by a grin just crooked enough and ears just jug enough to cast him as a corn-fed kid. In the fading sunlight, Smiley has yet to remove his sunglasses, and they conceal the most striking feature of all: two luminous blue eyes. Smiley is a decorated soldier whose war experience has received a lot of press coverage, and invariably the photographers focus on those beautiful eyes. The eyes are not real. Smiley wears them as much for us as for himself. When he steps off toward the mountaintop tonight it will be dark, but Smiley has grown used to dark. In 2005, while on patrol in Mosul, Iraq, Smiley spotted a car that squatted low to the ground. The driver was motionless behind the wheel. Suspecting the car was loaded with explosives, Smiley

4

considered shooting him, but nothing is certain, so he hollered
and fired warning shots. "The driver slowly raised both hands,"
says Smiley, "and then the car just disappeared." Shrapnel drove
into Smiley's head. One eye was gone, and the other was blinded.
The right side of his body was paralyzed. The medics who took
him in figured he wouldn't make it. He was still in his hospital bed
when a social worker suggested his wife should sign the papers
necessary to have him discharged. She refused.

Rehabilitation commenced almost immediately. Over time,
the paralysis receded. He learned to walk again. He carried a
piece of his skull around in his abdomen while his brain mended,
only to see the bone discarded and the gap filled with acrylic.
He hoped his right eye might be repaired, but it didn't happen.
He set about learning Braille and how to walk with a white stick.

And he stayed in the army—helping others drive an evolution in military policy that is beginning to regard the wounded
soldier not as a limited resource to be jettisoned but as someone
uniquely prepared to serve the mission in other capacities.

One year after his injury, Smiley was assigned to Army Ac-
cessions Command, helping to prepare new soldiers and their
families for the transition from civilian to military life. Now he
is obtaining his MBA from Duke University in preparation for a
career as a professor at West Point. If he makes it to the top of the
mountain tomorrow, he will have to hustle back down, because
on the following evening he is due in Washington, DC, to be recognized as the *Army Times* Soldier of the Year.

Ed Salau and Scott Smiley have come to the mountain hoping
other soldiers will follow. Smiley is here at the behest of Micah
Clark, executive director of Camp Patriot, a nascent nonprofit intended to arrange for volunteer guides to take disabled veterans
on outdoor adventures, and Salau is representing the Wounded
Warrior Project (WWP), an organization he first encountered
when representatives delivered a backpack of toiletries to him

bedside at Walter Reed. Five weeks later, they took him downhill skiing. "I didn't even have my prosthetic leg yet, and I was going fast," he says. "My kids looked at me and they were thinking, 'Hey, Dad's back!'"

A New Jersey native, Salau went straight into the Marine Corps after graduating in the bottom 5 percent of his high school class, completing boot camp 21 days before his 18th birthday. His service earned him a college education, and he found work as an occupational safety and health specialist. The position was still waiting for him when he returned from Iraq. "I stayed on for a while," he says, "but after the combat and rehab, the desk job wasn't a good fit." In February 2006, he joined the staff of WWP, where his responsibilities include management of an adaptive sports program for wounded soldiers.

The point, he says, is not just to take veterans on a hike, but to help them reengage the world. "I lost a leg, but I had an MBA and a job. I kept thinking of all these kids in my command, 19-year-olds who came straight from some small town or inner city, often from difficult circumstances, without the best academic background. They don't know what they're capable of in the first place; then they get hurt and suddenly they're back home looking in the mirror thinking they are less of a person. That's why I go to work."

"Let's go, Art!" says Ed Salau, feigning irritation. "Standing is the worst thing an amputee can do!" We are going back in time, to the first day of the climb. Sunday morning. July, and sunny. Guides Art Rausch, Curtis Fawley (121 summits of Rainier, and filming on this trip), and Ashley Garman are making last-minute preparations outside the Paradise visitor center. Salau knows he's in for a long haul, but at least when he's moving the pressure on his stump shifts. Too much compression in one area, for too long, produces a painful spot that can go raw and become infected. Rausch gives the go-ahead; Salau leads out. He's still on the paved trail and within earshot of the parking lot when he falls. The plastic boot on his prosthetic foot scuffed the asphalt and over he went. Crutches, backpack, the whole works. A small group of dayhikers rubbernecks as he struggles to stand. "When I was learning to walk again, I wasn't afraid of falling," he says. "I was afraid of people seeing me fall. It was a pride factor. Now I tell people there are two kinds of amputees—those who have fallen, and those who will fall again. You know, get over it. It's going to happen."

He's back on his feet now (his *foot* now, you think), back at the head of the line. Planting those crutches, trying to get the angle on how to best swing that heavy boot. He meets a steady counterflow of pedestrians, and invariably it's eyes straight ahead until he's past, then the heads spin and the murmuring begins. It's natural enough: To see a line of men headed for a mountain and one of them missing a leg and feel the need to comment. Some give him an *attaboy*. To which Scott Smiley responds, "Who's that?" and Curtis Fawley explains. Everyone notices the man with one leg, but Smiley is just another guy in sunglasses. Fawley has three miniature jingle bells attached to his backpack with a plastic zip-tie. The plan was for Smiley to follow the sound, but the bells don't jingle unless Fawley reaches around and tickles them, so instead he has taken to clicking his climbing poles together behind his legs. Micah Clark is close on Smiley's heels, watching his boots intently, giving him play-by-play. "Rock to your right . . . straight ahead now . . . more to your left . . ." Smiley hikes impassively for a good long stretch. He keeps his face oriented directly to the fore. If you have time to study him, you'll see he never looks down, which doesn't strike you as unusual until you notice it. Each foot hesitates just prior to touchdown, that extra millisecond allowing the nerves to give the brain the lay of the land. Now and then his boot strikes toe-first with a plasticky thump.

"To your left, Scotty," says Clark.

"Micah, you're gonna have to stop talking," says Smiley. "You'll be worn out before we get up this mountain." You can hear the grin in his voice, the timbre that's unexpectedly boyish and light in comparison to his stature and experience.

The peak is far above, and the group is still walking on asphalt. But behind them, Paradise drops away. Off to the left, on the other side of the Wapowety Cleaver, Van Trump Park is a cauldron of rolling mist. Already you can see for miles and miles.

Within an hour, the group reaches its first snow at around 5,600 feet. "We'll break here, guys," says Art Rausch. Salau steps into the snow and tips over. The climbing boot is just too clunky. After Salau gets himself upright and seated on his pack, Rausch kneels and removes the boot. "Let's try something different," he says, stripping the sock away to reveal a tan plastic foot that looks—right down to its sculpted toes—like it was filched from a department store mannequin. This "foot shell" slips over the actual weight-bearing base of the prosthesis to provide an anatomical fit inside a boot or shoe. The image of Salau eating a candy bar with one bare foot plonked in the snow makes the other climbers giggle. "Maybe the crampon," says Rausch, unrigging a pair from Salau's pack. Salau detaches his prosthesis at the knee and hands it to Rausch, who straps the crampon to the foot. He has to modify the perforated adjustment plate, and Salau gives a campy wince as Rausch uses a pair of multitool pliers to crimp the cold steel around the flesh-toned heel. Salau reattaches the leg and stands to check the balance: better. It's a distinctive look: one orange climbing boot and one nude-footed Franken-sandal. There are snow crystals on his toenails.

The break ends. The men shoulder their packs, taking a moment to squint across the snowfield and up the Nisqually Glacier all the way to the summit, brown and white against the blue sky. They are mountain climbers. Salau leads the way back to the trail, pausing a moment to let pass a pair of chubby first-graders in flip-flops. There is a ways to go.

A point of semantics: First Lieutenant Ed Salau did not lose his leg. Tough to lose your leg, he will point out, when it is strapped across your sternum, just six inches below your chin. Standard military procedure. The leg was apocalyptically detached, but it was not lost. That would come later, when the docs determined the damage was irreversible. From the day he got his orders for Iraq, he knew he might be killed or wounded. "I had accepted that," he says. "But I was a runner. I trained hard, and I ran for fun. And I do remember thinking, 'As long as nothing happens to my legs . . .'"

He was leading the platoon home from a patrol. It was getting dark. He was on lookout, standing in the turret of a Bradley fighting vehicle. "Head on a swivel," he says. "Look left, look right, look . . . *there he is.*" The first grenade was already on its way. It slammed into the vehicle, shattering the armor plating. The second grenade hit in the same spot, penetrating the vehicle, taking off Salau's leg and that of his gunner. First chance, he stuck his hands down his pants to make sure he had his gonads. "You're good, sir," said the medic attending him. Still bleeding, and he was already learning to recalibrate the standard for positive developments.

He's up there now, on point, humping along. Viewed from the rear, the backpacks ride high in a neat stair-stepped file, but every time Ed swings that leg through, his pack wags off-kilter like a shoulder-mounted metronome. Tick by tock, the cumulative lateral movement ratchets up his workload. The trail has turned gravelly and uneven. He's sweating. A breeze crosses the snow and cools his face. Rausch has had him redistribute a few items from his pack among the other climbers. His crampon grates in the shale. He is fighting for every foot of territory.

For his part, Scott Smiley is going pretty much unnoticed. Just stepping quietly along, tap-tapping his poles, sometimes using them like curb feelers to find larger stones beside the trail. Clark and Fawley cue him now and then, and in steeper rock jumbles he reaches ahead with his hands and sorts things out that way. He can feel the sun and then the breeze, hot and cool, and sometimes he smells the scent of fir trees. The other climbers feed him scenes now and then, describing how the treeline has given way to rocks and snow, how the clouds are skiffing past the peak, how his progress is being surveilled by a distant marmot. Off and on he has heard the sound of water, and now he hears it grow more insistent. It is time to cross Pebble Creek.

Salau goes first, and he's plenty nervous. It's not the rushing water, it's the fact that he has to teeter on these rocks. They drop sharply, and if he falls downhill he's going to take quite a crack. He's worried about gashing his face, smashing the prosthesis. He moves slowly, placing his crutches and plastic foot with great care, testing the stability, rock by rock. A misty fog has blown in. The stones are cold and gray. Once he commits to swinging his good leg through, he is an inverted pendulum, and all bets are off. "If I do fall," he says, "I hope to be knocked unconscious so I can feel the pain another day." Rausch, Fawley, and Garman triangulate, hovering around Salau, but keep their hands off. His lips are pinched with concentration. Rock to rock. The scrape of the crampon, the clunk of the boot. And then, the final pivot. The crampon bites into gravel and everyone blows out a breath of relief.

Smiley is more stable, but it takes him longer to place his sticks and feet. Clark holds his left arm, more to steady than to guide him. Garman follows close behind. Smiley crouches, and he places his sticks wide, like outriggers. When he completes the crossing, there are congratulations and smiles all around, but the cheerleading is contained. Everyone is working out the line between encouragement and patronization. After all, the men simply crossed a small creek.

It's a steep stretch now, up to a nearly vertical snowbank. Ed turns sideways, his prosthesis on the downside. Trading his upside pole for a shorter ice axe, he begins edging up, his left leg doing all the lifting while he drags the prosthesis. He grimaces with effort, his teeth in white contrast to his whisker stubble.

The snowbank is cut with chutes and troughs. Descending hikers choose chutes and slide down. Their wind pants pass over the granular snow with a high-pitched *zizzzz.* "What's that sound?" asks Smiley. It had not occurred to the rest of the crew to explain the sound. They had *seen* the sound.

At the next break, Rausch and Fawley huddle with Salau. He is redlining. At the current rate, it isn't at all clear that he can continue. Salau is disappointed, but he looks Rausch directly in the eye, and speaks crisply, militarily, matter-of-factly: "What are my options?" It's a question he's been asking ever since the grenade.

In the end, Rausch decides to redistribute the weight in his pack further. Everybody takes a few items. "Thanks, guys," says Salau. It's a tough moment. Tough for him to have to thank the team, even though every member would gladly take the man up the mountain piggyback. These are the things that go beyond losing your leg. Like having to hand stuff off to people. The snow is wet and grainy. When the grade allows, Salau faces forward and moves straight ahead. It seems to help when he steps in the footprint of the hiker preceding. But he is puffing out his cheeks now, on every breath.

Rausch steps in, helping Salau readjust the prosthesis. They are seeking the perfect uphill combination: knee locked, knee unlocked, sidestepping, whatever it takes. At one point, Salau swivels the plastic foot backward so it pivots off the heel rather than the toes. It's not the answer, but he leaves some confounding tracks. The sun is dropping. The peak is outlined against the sky. Salau leans into the slope and disappears over the ridge.

He is struggling. He is not stopping.

Salau and Smiley are not being offered up as pioneers: Blind climber Eric Weihenmayer summited Everest in 2001, double-amputee Mark Inglis in 2006. Rather, they are climbing to establish standards and realistic parameters for programs designed to serve a growing population of wounded vets. Each man has been asked to tell his story before—Smiley has addressed the United States men's Olympic basketball team, has been the focus of several media profiles, and is often called on to speak about his experience. (A devout Christian, he made his first postwar public appearance at his hometown church. "I basically bawled for 20 minutes," he says. "That was my speech.") Not everyone is inspired: Smiley's appearance with the basketball team spawned essays on *The Nation* and *Huffington Post* websites decrying the use of injured soldiers as a source of motivation.

Salau is not conflicted. "Those of us who have been visibly wounded have a responsibility to garner as much public awareness as we can for the overall needs of those who can't, or aren't listened to," he says. "Whether it's making the government enact proper legislation or create regulations that serve wounded from this war or 20 years ago, people like Scott build the awareness. This isn't just about taking guys waterskiing. I am proud of my country, but I am also proud of making sure it does right by its soldiers."

Behind the climbers the clouds are closing, and when next the men rest, they turn to see an otherworldly sight: a multimillion-acre comforter of spun sugar with Mount Adams poking through like you could swim to it. Farther west, Mount Saint Helens is a collapsed trifle. The sun drops behind the peak of Rainier, and the air chills immediately. When the climb resumes, it's just crunch and scuff—everybody working along, everyone in their own head. Time and altitude are adding up. The snow is dark blue.

The plan was to make Muir, but at the next rest stop Rausch points out the ridge that hides the base camp. "Think you can make it?" Salau looks upslope, then back at Rausch.

"No."

The group bivouacs at the edge of a snowfield. Passing by Salau, Micah Clark asks, "How you doin'?" "This is why God made ski lifts!" says Salau. Then he slaps the thigh of his foreshortened leg. "Touch it! You know you want to!" He's laughing and smartass-y, but his face is drawn. For his part, Smiley has been hiking right along, but when he takes a seat on his bedroll, it looks like he's down for good.

The guides are prepping dinner, and Salau and Smiley are left alone together for the first time all day. They fall into conversation, their voices a murmur behind the hiss of the gas jets and the soft *flap-flap* of water boiling. They are talking about the war now. When Smiley came back from Iraq, he was afraid to go out in public. Scared of everyone and anyone, he says. When he thinks of the war, he thinks of the heat and stink, the grit, cars honking, the rattle of his Stryker vehicle, the sound of explosions and small arms fire incoming. He likes the quiet up here on the snowfield.

Ed Salau took his first camping trip as a Boy Scout. Ever since, he says, whenever he had a sleeping bag and a backpack, he also had a rifle. He feels like this trip is bringing him full circle. Camping—and no bad guys. It's nice to just sit here, agrees Smiley, and not have to face outward.

The sunlight is all but gone, Rainier casting a final shadow across the clouds clear to Yakima. "There was this little town," says Salau. "Not a village, not quite a city. They had a two-story police station, and every day we made sure that the station wasn't bothered. The police chief looked to us for security. He knew we had the big guns. We became friends with the people. Spent time in their homes. After I was stateside, they told me a tanker truck pulled up one day. Leveled the building."

"We worked so *hard*," he says after a pause. "We worked so hard to keep them safe."

The food is ready. The headlamps cluster, dipping over reconstituted spaghetti. Everyone eats gratefully, the way people do in the cold out of doors after a hard day's slog.

Then there is the down-muffled whizz of sleeping bag zippers, and the shift of bodies settling. Bone-tired and concerned about contaminating the socket of his prosthesis, Salau detaches his foot but leaves the rest of the device in place. It's a calculated gamble. "Just like leaving my contacts in at night," he says. "You wake up in the morning and deal with what you've got."

And then it is quiet. Up above, the sky is shot with stars, the vaporous spray of the Milky Way spanning all creation. In the open air, Salau and Smiley sleep.

Come morning, the clouds have broken up and slipped downslope. The sky is blue, the sun is bright, and Muir is all but in sight. Ed Salau is reinvigorated. He has heard there is a handicapped-accessible restroom at Muir. "*That* I have got to see," he says. As with anything in the mountains, the camp is farther than it appears, but Salau is on a mission and pulls away. By the time he reaches the stone hut at Muir an hour later, the word has gone out—a ranger and a cluster of climbers are waiting with congratulations. Salau takes a moment to look back, and his first thought is, Holy crap, I just came up that thing! Then he goes hunting for the bathroom. Sure enough, a few rocky steps away he finds a unisex outhouse clearly marked with a blue wheelchair—and a sign that says CLOSED. "Nooo!" moans Salau in mock horror, posing for a picture beside the sign with his titanium leg bent backward.

Rejoining the rest of the group, Salau sits and begins to undo his prosthesis. Smiley is three feet away, relaxing with a snack. Turning his head in Salau's direction he grins and says, "Hey, this climbing business ain't that difficult." "Shut up, Scott," says Salau, removing his leg. For the first time in more than 24 hours, fresh air hits his stump. "Quit starin' at the nub!" he barks at no one in particular, and about six people avert their gaze. He chuckles. "You work up routines," he says. Necessary routines. "You'd be surprised," he says, "at how many strangers begin with the leg. 'What happened to your leg?' they say, so I just look at them and say, 'My name's Ed, who are you?'" He can change tack depending on the circumstance. "I was in the Dunkin' Donuts, and this little kid kept staring at my leg. His mom came over and apologized. I told her not to worry about it. At least little kids are honest about their curiosity. Then as they were leaving, she came over again and said the boy wanted to ask how I lost the leg. So I looked him right in the eye and said, 'Too much PlayStation.'"

He's looking the stump over now, checking for hot spots. The stump is rounded off, the leg muscle folded over the end of the bone and sealed with scars. There is some redness, but the skin is intact. To re-don the leg, Salau will encase the stump in a "pull sock"—essentially a nylon bag. After pushing the stump into the socket, he will extract the pull sock through a porthole, creating suction that holds the leg in place without straps. Drawback is, that socket can get pretty ripe. Fishing around in his pack, he produces an antiperspirant stick and waves it in the air. "Secret Platinum—strong enough for a man, made for an amputee."

Salau tells the rest of the story about the kid at the Dunkin' Donuts, and says when he finally gave the kid the straight answer, that he got hurt being a soldier, the kid looked at him and said, "I prayed for you," and he stops talking right there, and for the first time all climb, he has tears in his eyes.

Reaching into the pack again, he pulls out a hunk of yellow construction paper. It's folded into a homemade card—the first one he received after his wounding. It came from a girl named Elizabeth. He carries it everywhere, and it's creased some, but the bright red "thank you" splashed across the front remains bold. A Valentine-style heart is centered beneath the salutation and flanked by two smiling faces. Inside is drawn what appears to be a smoking pistol and the following inscription: *To soldier's for fiting are cuntrey.* Then another heart. And beneath that, another note: *Hope you fell beteter!*

"*Fell* better," he says. He loves that.

After lunch, Art Rausch turns into a drill sergeant, marching everyone up and down the slopes to practice rope work and re-hearse self-arrest. Over and over, he gives the command to fall, and every time, the climbers call out "FALLING!" so that the other members of the rope team have time to brace. Any falling climber relies on his partners, but for Smiley this will be especially crit-ical. He holds himself humped over his axe while Rausch makes the rounds, yanking hips up and pushing shoulders down, making the same rough adjustments as a football coach teaching the proper blocking stance. Salau is flopping to the snow right along with everyone else. He knows by now that he is going no higher and is in no mood, but he hopes the film Fawley is shooting will advance the program. At one point while he is prone, another climber kicks him in the head. It is understandable, then, that once the training concludes, he takes himself off to be alone. To stare off across those foothills and think about where he's been. Where he'll go.

Some who have lived it say the physical damage of combat is more readily adjusted to than the psychological. This raises the parallel question of whether such things can be repaired by a walk in the wilderness. Right now, Ed Salau could argue either way.

See him standing there? The Paradise parking lot sits somewhere in the neighborhood of 5,420 feet. Camp Muir is at 10,080. Salau has hiked four miles and 4,660 vertical feet. Divide that by your standard seven-inch stair riser, and he has climbed 7,989 stairs. Should you wish to re-create his experience, it will be instructive to prop a piece of plywood against the garage at a declivitous angle, clamber atop it, tie up one leg, and with the other, execute 7,989 lunges. After the first 5,000 or so, go ahead and drop your 40-pound backpack.

Then see who you pity.

Scott Smiley is in bed by 9 p.m. Two hours later, Art Rausch is tugging at his sleeping bag. "I'm not so sure I'm into these alpine wakeups," chuckles Smiley. Everyone assembles down by the cookstove. Two more guides—Andy Kittleson and Andres Marin—have joined the group. Kittleson will lead Smiley's team (with Rausch and Fawley fore and aft of Smiley), and Marin will lead the second group of writer, photographer, and Micah Clark. The teams gear up by the light of their headlamps. Little light-pools jerk and slide about to the tune of clinking carabiners, the *zup!* of harnesses being tightened, the crunch of boots in hard snow. Ashley Garman makes the rounds with beef stroganoff, ensuring everyone is fully dosed. The guides review gear one last time, then the teams step off around the cliff-sheltered bowl of the upper Cowlitz. Several other groups have already departed. Their headlamps dot the distance like abbreviated strings of Christmas lights.

The Cowlitz is a walk in the park, and then it's steeply up the switchback scree of Cathedral Gap. There is no snow here and Smiley can hear his crampons grinding against rocks. He's angled forward at the ankles. Already his calves are burning. It's doubly tough never knowing how his foot is going to land. While everyone else tilts their headlamps to the trail and picks their way, Smiley is walking blindfolded through a room full of bowling balls, none of the same size.

After the scramble up the gap, the Ingraham Flats are a relative stroll. Three-quarters of the way up, Rausch calls the first break. The heat of the climb sweeps away in a pressing wind. "Get your parkas on," says Rausch. Smiley feels a little something in the pit of his stomach—if that was an *easy* stretch, what's to come? "Parkas off," orders Rausch, and Kittleson leads out. A vertiginous smattering of constellations shifts in the sky above.

Headlamps.

The easy part is over.

Thousands of people attempt to climb to the summit of Mount Rainier every year, and roughly half of them are successful. There are many more technically difficult mountains in the country; Kittleson will be taking the most popular route to the top, and the good weather is likely to hold. Still, conditions on Rainier are famous for going to hell in a hurry, and every year a handful of climbers perish on the slopes. It's no Everest, but it's enough.

In 1981, right where Smiley is walking, a wall of snow and ice broke loose and buried 11 climbers forever. Fawley is guiding him across a series of crevasses, talking him right up to the edge, then having him reach across to gauge the distance with a ski pole. When he has the breadth in his head, he takes the big step. Anymore, he will tell you, he lives much of his life on trust.

After the crevasses, Kittleson paces the team up through Disappointment Cleaver, and Smiley is shortly believing the stretch is aptly named. Half the time he's nearly knee-walking, feeling his way up the rocky spine. Rausch and Fawley patiently coach his every step, their headlamps trained on his feet. Kittleson is constantly on guard, ready to drop and lock at the first sound of a slip. So early, and already Smiley is suffering. "My calves," he tells Rausch during a break. "They feel like they're about to blow up." "Tweak your foot placement," says Rausch. "Displace the strain to other muscles."

The team emerges from the Cleaver two hours later. Smiley is whipped. He sinks to the snow. Rausch and Fawley wrap him in his parka, and the three discuss the situation. "I don't think I can make it," Smiley says. "My calves . . ." Behind him the sky is becoming a bandshell of light, the rim of the earth molten orange. Smiley thinks he should turn back. "It's your decision," says Rausch, "but I really believe you can do this." Gentle but insistent, the guides have seen this before. "The Cleaver is your first real taste," says Fawley. "It's a psychological thing."

"One more section," says Smiley finally. "See how I feel." Overheated on the climb, he's shivering now. One of the climbing party eases up beside him to describe the sunrise. Smiley listens—what choice does he have—but you can see his head is elsewhere. Barely begun, and it's no fun anymore. In pushing Smiley, Rausch is making a calculated gamble. The ascent is going much slower than he and Fawley had hoped, and long before you make the summit, you must contemplate the descent. There is only so much time to get off the mountain. All signs are for a sunny day—that sounds good now, but melting ice and softening snow lead to dangerously unstable conditions, and Smiley is less stable than most.

For now, temperatures remain frigid. Andres Marin is parsing his team around the fissured blue maw of a prodigious crevasse, spreading them out along the rope as they approach a vanishingly narrow ice bridge. Stepping meticulously, Marin eases across the abyss and sets a picket, to which he secures a line so that the other climbers can clip in for the crossing. Clark is next across. Kneeling to unclip, he loses hold of his ice axe. It rattles across the ice and does a slow-motion gainer into the crevasse. Smiley and his team have caught up now, and after the axe drops from sight, everyone remains frozen for a beat, ears cocked for a ping or clang. Nothing.

Fawley clips Smiley to the fixed line and begins to coach him across the span. For fear of overloading the bridge, the two guides have to let Smiley go solo. The ice axe incident has left everyone a little edgy. Smiley puts one foot before the other in super slow motion. "Keep feeling that uphill edge, Scotty," says Fawley. He tries for an even tone, but Smiley detects the tension. When he lost his sight, his fear of heights went with it, and it's a good thing. The ice along the chasm lip is heaved and tumbled, and the aquamarine void beneath him seems cut to the very core of the earth.

He makes it across to a relatively flat traverse, and everyone exhales. There are no more rocks or crevasses between here and the summit. Just snow. But from here on, it's unrelentingly upward, and the air is getting rare. Five minutes into the next leg, Smiley and the other unacclimated members of the group are huffing like emphysema patients, and Smiley is back to suffering. The constant stress of having to balance without visual cues has spread to his abs and back and arms—everything taut and sore— and now the thin air has put his pulse to pounding in his head. Think through it, he tells himself. My feet, he thinks. My calves.

And more to the point: Why did I say yes to this? Break after break, he is sure he won't continue. The pitch is so steep Fawley and Rausch have warned him not to set his water bottle on the snow or it will slide off to some couloir thousands of feet below. Each time, he catches his breath just enough to tell Rausch he'll go one more. He is on autopilot.

The sun is well up when Marin's group summits. Turning, they drop their packs and sit, watching for Smiley. He will be hidden until the final switchback. Last they saw him, Smiley wasn't talking, all his energy devoted to putting one foot before the other. Another party of climbers celebrates boisterously, but Marin's group is quiet, eyes fixed on the final switchback. At some point during the climb, each person has closed his eyes for a step or two, just to get a sense. The vertigo comes on fast, like a shove on the shoulder. Your hand shoots out, you drop your center of gravity, your eyes snap open. Given a sliver of Scott Smiley's life, you opt out.

And there he is now.

"Aw'right, Scotty!"

"Y'got it, bud!"

He comes on steadily, just as he has since the trailhead at Paradise. Twenty yards . . . 15 . . . 10 . . . The persistent pace, the strong, implacable face. Kittleson and Fawley coil the line as he closes the gap, but they do not pull him. Down at Muir, Smiley had taken Rausch aside: "Make it or not, let me climb this thing myself. I don't want be a football."

"You made it, Scotty," says Fawley, and he guides Smiley to the ground, where he sits with a big loose-mouthed grin, his tongue at a comical loll. Smiley came of age in nearby Pasco and spent a good chunk of his army career at Fort Lewis, so he carries a clear image of Rainier and can conjure a picture of himself atop the blazing white peak, high above the curve of the world. Turning to the video camera, he says he loves his wife, and he says he is thinking of Ed. He says he would have given up if Art hadn't pushed him.

The sun is brilliant. Down below, the melt is on.

It's time to go.

The descent is a whole new sort of trouble. In the time since Smiley summited, the snow has gone slushy. After the first couple of switchbacks, it clogs his crampons and turns his boots into size 10 snowboards. "Jam your foot heel-first in the snow," Rausch reminds him, but it's tough, not being able to read the angle of the slope first. He falls, then falls again. Nothing spectacular, he just drops to his knees, but then he has to lurch upright, reposition his ice axe, get oriented, and take the next step. Jam, jam, slide. Jam, jam, slide. He senses all of the free-fall air to the downslope side and worries that one of these times he will plunge and drag the entire team down with him. At every switchback, he swaps his axe to his upslope hand, repeating the position of self-arrest until it becomes reflex.

By the time he reaches the ice bridge, it has deteriorated to the point that Marin has cut a new path between two monstrous parallel crevasses, one of which calves a chunk of ice the size of a city bus right when the team is strung out on the rope. Smiley can hear the chunks breaking loose. It is a nerve-wracking stretch, and just when Fawley tells him the diciest portion is past, he hears a distant rumble. Rausch pauses, and Smiley, feeling the rope go taut, stops. The rumble is swelling—an avalanche? Smiley can hear Micah Clark, hollering from several hundred feet below.

"Scotty! Scotty! The jets!"

There are four F-16s, formed up tight, carving a vast curve around the mountain. Clark arranged the salute, and up to this minute he wasn't sure it would happen. Flat gray and solid in the sky, the jets hiss past at what seems eye level or a little below, and then they are gone, and a raven drifts up the Emmons Glacier.

The fly-by gives everyone a boost, but soon it's back to the slog. The snow is ever slushier, and when he walks close to the crevasse edges, Smiley can hear the trickling melt. Time and time again he falls to his knees, time and time again he stands and resumes hiking. Two hours into the descent, Kittleson stops the group.

"Disappointment Cleaver, Scotty," says Rausch. As he starts down, Smiley remembers he was ready to quit here. It seems a week ago, and maybe he relaxes a little, because suddenly he is sliding and his feet shoot out and there is only air and just like he trained he announces, "Falling!" Only he says it in that young boy voice, calm as if he is excusing himself from the dinner table. He whirls and tries to get into self-arrest position, but when he comes to a stop he is sideways, suspended in the vee of the rope, ice axe scratching the snow.

"Okay, Scotty, okay, we've got you, you're good." Rausch and Fawley are holding rock-solid, but there is a pitch to their voices. Smiley is dangling 500 feet above the next switchback. A few stones have rattled off and scattered across the snow far below. With Kittleson on anchor, Rausch and Fawley reel the big soldier in, draw him back to the trail, help him to his feet. And then Kittleson leads out again. There is no shortcut home. No *survivable* shortcut.

Ed Salau has been scanning Cathedral Gap for hours before Smiley appears. When news comes ahead that he made the summit, Salau is elated. An hour later, everyone is circled up, sitting on packs and snowbanks, jabbering. Smiley removes his boots and socks and says it's the finest thing he's felt since leaving camp. Describing the Cleaver descent to Salau, Smiley says, "I guess I fell in a trough or something," and the other climbers hoot when they realize he has no idea. Salau tells the best one-legged story ever, about the time he went out wearing shorts and sandals and his cosmetic leg—the one made by the same people who do dead bodies for the CSI television shows, the one with actual toe hair shaved from his right leg—and when this drunk lady kept pestering him he surreptitiously hit the swivel button and walked a complete circle around his fake foot while it stayed planted, at which point the woman barfed and ran from the bar.

Apart from the group, the guides are visibly relieved. Fawley says this is the most memorable climb since his first, the one with his father. "These guys . . ." says Rausch, and then he can't continue. It takes him a while, then he says, "I don't carry anybody up that mountain. But to see them . . ." He trails off again. "I'm in the reserves. I got deployed in 2004 to Qatar. I've never been in harm's way. These guys . . . it just cuts me up. I'd carry . . . I'd carry everything for them."

The descent to Paradise remains. Fawley and Kittleson will escort Smiley down tonight so he can make his plane, and Salau will descend in the morning. More of the same, in reverse. But at this moment, the group vibrates with the shared euphoria of hazard and hardship overcome in a place far removed from civilization and its various complications. Adversity runs a sliding scale— elective nature hikes at the low end, Salau's leg and Smiley's eyes at the unthinkable high end—but even a hill climb such as this can kick irony in the slats and give despair the raspberries.

Mount Rainier is a volcano, of course. Ed Salau didn't get there, and Scott Smiley couldn't see it, but the summit is a vast white bowl. A crucible, you could say, from which hope might be forged.

2008

MY DAUGHTER'S FATHER

I am paying for two tickets to a local production of *You're a Good Man, Charlie Brown* when the lady behind the ticket counter leans out and looks down at the little blue-eyed girl holding my hand. "It sure is nice of your daddy to bring you to a play!"

I know what's coming next.

"He's not my daddy."

Now the ticket lady is nervous and apologetic. I have lived this moment before. This is the part where the grown-ups tend to sweat and shuffle, or launch into backpedaling babble. The five-year-old, of course, is just standing there fully committed to honesty and full disclosure.

The day I met my wife, Anneliese, I met her daughter, Amy. Anneliese and I met by chance at the library, which led to a date, which led to more dates, and the day we were married Amy was four years old. Now Amy is five, and we are well into our lives together. I have helped her learn to ride a bike, half-taught her to tie her shoes (mom finished the job), and recently took my turn on the midnight shift when she developed a bladder infection. The next day Anneliese took Amy to the clinic for tests. When the nurse called with the results, I was home alone.

"Mr. Scherer?" Amy and her mother share the same last name, and kept it when we were married.

"This is Mrs. Scherer's husband." I explained that Anneliese was not home and asked how the test turned out.

"I'm sorry, I can only share those results with a legal guardian."
Wow. Didn't see that one coming.

Amy's daddy—her biological father, that is—lives in Colorado.
His name is Dan and sometimes Amy sits on my lap and we send
him e-mails. She dictates and I type. Amy likes to draw pictures.
"This one is for you," she'll say, and then she watches to be sure
I tape it to the wall beside my desk. Later she brings another one.
"This one is for Daddy." We put it in the scanner and shoot it from
Wisconsin to the Rockies in an instant. There are phone calls and
cards back and forth, and once or twice a year he comes to visit
us or we go to visit him.

Dan is with me constantly through Amy. The way she sleeps
with her head under the blankets—Dan tells me he has slept that
way since he was a child. Dan is the shortest of three brothers
at 6 foot 7. Amy's aunt is 6 foot 2. I am 5 foot 8. Amy is five years
old, and nearly as tall as my sternum. I figure I will tower above
her until she is 11.

One night after supper, I play guitar and sing some songs.
Amy has her own guitar. She doesn't know any chords, but she
gets the rhythm and lyrics right. At one point she stops playing,
looks up at me, and says, "I want to sing and play with you for all
my life." You could have lit Manhattan with the glow that rose in
my chest. A short while later she picks up the picture of her and
Dan from the bedside stand and there are tears in her eyes. The
glow in my chest turns to a lump in my throat. I get her crayons
and tell her if she draws a picture, I will send it. She chooses a
bright yellow piece of paper. Everyone she draws—even the dog
that looks like a tick—is smiling.

The only time Amy calls me "Dad" is when she has friends
visiting. I suspect she wants to fit in. Mostly she calls me Mike,
and I think it's fine. But the thing that's toughest—I guess I should
say so far—is not knowing how to handle the "Daddy" thing in

public. Sometimes I don't know how to refer to her in front of her. If I say she is my daughter, she may quite innocently—and rightly—contradict me. If I don't claim her as my daughter, I may be hurting her. Lately I am toying with the idea of saying, "Yes, I met her when she was three years old and now her mommy and I are married."

With Amy, my wife says, she is less concerned with form than function. "Regardless of what she calls you," she said, "I expect you to provide her with a father *figure.*" Meaning, when it comes to parenting, my active presence is more relevant than my title. After four years of being a single mom, she wants a partner in the day-to-day business of parenting—from the high-minded (demonstrating loving, respectful behavior) to the fundamental (splitting the good cop/bad cop duties).

And, of course, some assistance in addressing the meaning of life. Six months ago Amy asked me if God was real. I'm a waffling agnostic, but I figured, "Well, I sure hope so," or "Here's my copy of *Being and Nothingness,*" didn't constitute responsible answers. My stammering was worsened by the fact that Amy's father is a principled Catholic. In true agnostic style, I equivocated: "A lot of people think so." Dan and I have agreed we will speak honestly to Amy about our beliefs and let her arrive at her own informed decision, but I wonder sometimes who will pay the price for contradictions in the name of open-mindedness: me, him, or her.

From spirituality to spankings, the absent father is always in your back pocket. Last year I was holding Amy's hand as we walked through a village carnival in Mexico. She was pouting because her mother had gone ahead with friends. Suddenly Amy pulled her hand from mine and bolted. In a heartbeat, she was six feet away and bodies were closing around her. I dove after her, grabbed her arm, and gave her a swat, as much out of fear as anger. When I mentioned this to a friend, he said if he spanked his stepchild he would face a lawsuit from the biological father.

And so Dan and I have had the spanking talk. As it turns out, we both feel the judicious swat (as opposed to angry thrashing, and accompanied by the appropriate mind-numbing sermon for context) is a legitimate tool, although outside of that night in Mexico I have yet to use it. But we've agreed on the ground rules.

Still, even when both of you are doing your best to do right for the child, there is room for suspicion. Every time Dan's support check arrives, I wonder if he thinks I'm a freeloading slob for including it in our family budget. On a darker level, having been witness to situations in which the custody battle was as much over the check as the child, I sometimes catch myself wondering if today's payment will be used as a claim against future returns. When Amy's bladder infection recurred, my wife and I debated whether we should subject her to additional medical tests. Doctors gave us conflicting advice, but a part of me wanted the tests just to prove to her father that we were being vigilant. Every parent dreads doing the wrong thing, but you dread it doubly if you think the third parent may hold it over or against you. Step-parenting has a way of sprouting the smallest seeds of paranoia.

Amy's father says he and I are an anomaly relying on grace and friendship. The situation is fraught with alpha-male tinder, but so far, so good. We work steadily at that old relationship chestnut, communication. When I was bothered about the child support check, I brought it up. During the bladder infection saga, my wife recalled Dan mentioning a childhood episode requiring surgery, which resulted in he and I exchanging e-mails about the state of his urethra, which is not the kind of thing you necessarily sign up for. We've figured out it is pretty much up to us to define our roles, the caveat being that you can only control one half of an equation that will skew to the lowest common denominator of dysfunction. In this I am blessed in that Dan is a good, intelligent, and responsible man.

Make no mistake: Neither Amy's father nor I are pretending that this is some sort of delightful alternative lifestyle adventure with no downside. For all the nervous freight attached to the idea of meeting the parents of your fiancée, it really doesn't hold a candle to meeting the man with whom she has conceived a child. You may be sitting at breakfast together in his house, pleased with your maturity and progressiveness, but at some point, even under the best of circumstances, you will not enjoy thinking about all he and your wife share. What we do understand is this is our reality, and the courts are crammed with realities immeasurably worse. We understand our roles, we understand our responsibilities, and working from that, we craft this relationship.

Only one person will know for sure if we are successful. Last week Amy learned to ride her bicycle. After several weeks of jogging behind her holding the seat, feeling her veer left and right with no sense of balance, all of a sudden I felt the bike center, and for one, two, three revolutions of the pedal, she had it. She looked back then, to see where I was, and of course tipped over. But on the very next try, I let go, and she pedaled away, wobbling and veering, but pulling away, all on her own.

I was proud. Silly proud. Got a little misty, for Pete's sake. And when she put the bike away for the night, I picked her up, looked her in the eyes and was happy to say, "Let's call Daddy."

2005

P.S. Today she is six feet tall.

MUSHING

Above all, you are humbled by the dogs. They are up there tugging, heads bobbling like Ping-Pong balls on a vibrating motel bed, lugging your lard up, down, and around the frozen wilds of northern Minnesota, while you merely offer encouragement from the back of a sled lumbered with the equipment required to coddle and keep you alive through the subzero nights. The dogs, of course, will simply curl up in the snow, tuck their noses beneath their tails, and wait for morning, when they will lug you again.

Make no mistake: The dogs are happy to pull. To believe otherwise is to remain willfully blind to their demeanor. Perhaps because I was raised on a farm where my father taught us to treat animals with respect but not confuse them with long-term family members, I am not one to get anthropomorphic. And yet, when we pull off trail for a cheese and hot cider break, I feel compelled to move from wheel dog to lead dog, kneeling to pat and scratch each one, looking into their eyes in an attempt to convey gratitude.

When it is time to run again, I step to the back of the sled and, with one foot on the rail and one on the brake, say, "Ready?" The dogs jump up and lean eagerly to harness, tails wagging. I wait, and they glance back over their shoulders. "Ready?" I say again, in the tone I might use before giving a child a push on a swing. The dogs whine and stamp their feet, and the tug line tightens.

"All right," I say, and release the brake. We fly away into the woods.

• • •

"Mushing," says Arleigh Jorgenson, "is a natural skill, not a technical skill." Arleigh, 59, is a former seminarian whose windburned cheeks reflect 30 years on a sled. We are standing in the bright winter sun surrounded by barking huskies and he is appraising me with that gaze self-reliant folk reserve for the softer members of civilization. "You have to think like a dog."

Arleigh's tone is gentle, but the implication remains an open question. Long ago, inspired by pictures in a *National Geographic* article on Eskimos, I forced my little brother to pull me around the yard on a toboggan. This was unsatisfying, and I've wanted to experience a sled pulled by real dogs ever since. Cross-country skiing has never been an adequate replacement. I'm not coordinated and find trying to ski like trying to dance. The results are humiliating and sweaty, and all the graceful people keep telling me it's easy, which makes me think I should be allowed to run them through with the poles I won't need anymore *now that I've stabbed you to death on the trail because you wouldn't listen.* So I was eager to join Arleigh, who runs a sled-dog outfit, for a three-day trip into the Superior National Forest, in northeastern Minnesota. I signed up to drive a team of six dogs.

"Your job is to keep the tug line straight," says Arleigh, pointing down the long axis of the sled where six dogs stand hitched to either side of a plastic-coated cable. "Use the brake to keep a little tension in it. If you slow them down a little now and then, they get frustrated and pull harder. If the line goes slack, they tend to let up. This is especially important coming off hills—if you overtake the team, you're going to hurt one of my dogs." His voice is still gentle, but his eyes sharpen when he says *my dogs,* and you can imagine what it would feel like to have that sled bumper slam you in the ankles a few times before Arleigh unclips you to walk home 40 miles through the wilderness with a granola bar and a safety match. "Downhill is where the dogs learn to trust you," he says. "Now go hold your leaders. Get to know them."

I walk up the line and face the two dogs yoked to the front. "Hans and Fittipaldi," says Arleigh's son, Odin, who at 27 has already perfected his father's steady gaze. "Hans is a good lead, but he has a habit of stopping to sniff and pee on bushes." I pet and talk to both dogs. They endure the attention politely, but keep looking over my shoulder at Odin and Arleigh packing the lead sled. If you've ever been at a cocktail party talking to someone who glances away every time someone popular enters the room, you get the idea.

The yard is full of dogs, some standing atop their plastic shelters, some straining against their chains, some whining, some barking a baritone *r'uh, r'uh, r'uh*, others howling *yow, yowp-yow!* Most are smaller to midsized Alaskan Huskies with bloodlines traceable to northern Canada, although Arleigh says nowadays the geographical elements of breeding are more a reflection of a dog's abilities than its place of birth. "These are bred for racing," he says. "Bred to be 40 or 50 pounds. Bigger dogs are better for pulling heavy loads, but they can't run as far, or as fast, and they won't push the pace." Arleigh says he tried breeding some greyhound blood into the line once. "All I got was village dogs," he says. He doesn't explain, but from the tone of his voice it is clear: You do not want to be a village dog.

Once you go, you go. There is no buildup. Arleigh's sled is moving off ahead, and my dogs leap to the traces. The dogs left tethered in the yard set up a howl and holler, and just as quickly—*zip*—it is just you and your team whooshing through a tunnel of spruce. The runners hiss against the snow, and the cargo bay grunts and creaks as the straps ease and the load settles. I keep my right foot on the studded rubber flap of the drag brake, but the dogs are flat-out flying. The first corner approaches, and now I realize why Arleigh puts your focus on that tug line. Any more responsibility at this speed this early, and you'd bail out at the first bend. "Slow 'em down on the straightaways and let 'em go on the corners," he'd said. It's counterintuitive, but if you brake on the corner, the dogs drag you straight into the brush. I step off the brake and hope for the best. The dogs stream around a tree trunk and out of sight. I dip, lean, and shift my weight. The sled tail kicks out and sweeps through the corner in an arc, tracking neatly in the dogs' wake. The tree is scarred by beginners who gave in to the temptation of braking.

The trail winds through a dense forest near the upper meadows of the Kadunce River. It is a full-time job to cycle the checklist: Watch the cable, duck branches, scan for corners, watch the cable, duck, cable, *duck!* I "pedal" some on the uphills, dropping a foot to push and take some weight off the sled. When the dogs hear your boot thumping the snow, they look back with tongue-lolling grins, then pull even harder—although Odin says if you help too much, they will get lazy. They also look back if you overplay the drag brake or bump a tree and jerk the cable, clearly wondering how humans reached the top of the food chain.

By midmorning, as predicted, Hans is distracted by the bushes, and Odin pulls up. "I'm gonna change him out," he says. He switches Hans with a small dog named Abner. "Lead dogs have egos—if I move Hans back, he'll work hard to get back out front." The uptick in pace is remarkable—as if Odin swapped out a fouled spark plug.

I am fascinated by each dog's distinct character. In the wheel position, a husky named Buck runs while shouldering hard to the right against Reese, the largest dog on my team, who runs like a veteran jock—pulling his weight, but never breaking out of a lope if he can help it. Oliva, now partnered with Hans in the middle position, ducks shyly when I pet her but lunges forward when it's time to pull. Out front, Fittipaldi presses the harness, running hard, fast, and arrow-straight, feet a pitter-pat blur. And Abner—Abner is frantic in his desire to pull, running with his tiny body rotated 20 degrees off center and his backbone hunched, directing all his force against his right shoulder. Looking like he's half-cocked to take a dump, he goes and goes.

Mushing is organic snowmobiling. Enough speed to feed your appetite for new territory, without the piston-blast. Because you can hear the sled's squeak and the dog paws drumming, you feel not so much that you are covering ground as flowing the terrain. You learn to roll against the flex of the runners, and soon you are slow-dancing the curve of the earth. We run all morning, stop for lunch, then run again. We descend, break through the dogwood brush flats, and plane out across the smooth ice of the Brule River.

That night we camp in a tight stand of spruce. First we unharness the dogs and string them boy-girl along a drop line. Each gets a bit of straw on which to bed, and while they roll and settle I trail Odin back to the river. He chunks a hole through two feet of ice with a steel spud, then we ladle water into pails, dipping slowly to avoid stirring up the silt. We pass the time discussing his senior thesis: *Gloom, Despair, and Agony: A Comparison of Soren Kierkegaard and Dzogchen Buddhist Teachings Concerning Questions of Existential Despair and Suffering.* After a brief consultation, we decided to go on living. Above us, the stars emerge.

Back at camp, Odin heats the water on a camp stove, then pours it over buckets of kibble. "Sneaks water into their system," he says. "If you give them straight water, they won't drink enough." After the steaming paste is ladled out into battered steel pans, we set up camp, eat, then drink coffee and talk big ideas until the coals have put a hole three feet deep in the snow. When you mush with a philosopher who has been running sled dogs for three decades and another who is capable of synthesizing Scandinavian existentialism, Tibetan Buddhism, and a song from *Hee-Haw,* you need not pass the time lighting farts. At one point, we are interrupted when every dog on the line springs up and sets to howling. The phase-shifting, ululating swirl fills the forest, and I am spooked and delighted. Later, when I emerge from the insulated tent to pee at three a.m., the air is subzero still, the campsite snow is striped with tree-trunk moonshadow, and each dog is a coiled furry circle.

◆ ◆ ◆

At breakfast, the spruce are shot through with sunbeams that illuminate stray snowflakes as they filter through the canopy. The dogs are lapping up kibble broth as we eat French toast beneath the opportunistic gaze of a whiskey jack. We fold the camp, load the sleds, hook up the dogs, and slide away. The trees are lofted with snow and every sound is muffled. We spend much of the day mushing through rolling woodlands and recovering clear-cuts. The sun is warm on my nose. If I do get cold, I just pedal some. The dogs become a thicket of tails.

By afternoon, we are dropping rapidly through big trees. I nearly lose it two switchbacks in a row, then suddenly we pop out on the broad plain of Esther Lake. The sled bumper fluffs through the unspoiled feather-pillow snow. White pines stand windblown on the skyline, and a bald eagle watches from a snag. Twenty-five miles today. We make camp at the lake's far end, at the base of a sheer rock face. When the dogs howl in the night, the primordial sound echoes off the palisade.

The first thing I hear on our final day is snow sliding from the tent. It falls thickly that morning, even when the sun blazes. The effect is blinding and beautiful. I feel so comfortable on the sled that I relax and get dumped on a downhill corner. I run after the dogs, shouting *whoa, whoa, whoa!*—a backsliding existentialist unwilling to trade the sled for the void. I catch them only because they are struggling to drag the sled up the hill sideways.

We bite off a long run—more than 30 miles—and Arleigh pushes hard to get us in by nightfall, but I don't want the ride to end. We shoot through the forested half-light, plaiting ourselves between the gray tree trunks in pure cold silence, snaky wraiths working our way back to civilization. Finally, I hear the yard dogs howling, and the sled jumps a little as Abner and the others dig for home.

2006

MIKE IS A NURSE

There is a thing called a "kill fee." It is the money you are paid if you write a piece for a magazine and then they decide not to print it. Usually it runs around 25 percent of what you were gonna get. This piece got killed and it's probably for the best, because there are passages in here that make the older (I hope more thoughtful) me wince. Also, parts of it read like a job fair brochure. But there are also passages that make me smile, and make me grateful. Fact remains, 28 years ago I decided to try writing for a living. I figured if it all flopped, I could go back to nursing. That's still the plan.

There came a day when I decided to tell my father I wanted to be a nurse. Dad is a quiet, hardworking farmer. I caught him on the way to the barn. We stood there in the dirt driveway. "Dad," I said, "I wanna be a nurse."

There was a beat, then he said, "Well, your mother's a nurse." This was approval. My mother is my father's best friend. Dad spoke again. "I think you'll make a fine nurse." He turned and began walking back toward the barn, but then he stopped, and started back. "Just one thing . . ."

Oh boy, I thought, here it comes.

"I just wanna be there when they pin that little white cap on ya!"

● ● ●

The very term "male nurse" comes prepackaged with its own set of wisecracks. If you saw *Meet the Parents* you get the idea. I put myself through nursing school by working on a cattle ranch in Wyoming. My cowboy buddies used to propose untoward scenarios involving bedpans, sponge baths, and backrub lotion—I have since come to believe they were working through a few issues of their own. Things weren't much different at nursing school. On my first day of classes, I found a line of graffiti in the men's locker room—*male nurses are homos.* I remember examining the cramped script and thinking I could kick the crap out of the guy who wrote that. Not the most enlightened response, but so it goes when you mix your cowboying and your nursing.

At every opportunity, I did my level best to broaden public perceptions of the profession. One day after class, I went to visit my goddaughter in the hospital. Her large family—a rough-and-tumble clan from my rural hometown—was gathered around the room. I mentioned that I'd just come from nursing school, and Grandpa—a patriarch of World War II vintage—made some crack implying that I might be in it for the white nylons. I drew myself up and launched into an extended disquisition on the history of men in nursing (the all-male Knights Hospitalers of St. John of Jerusalem could palpate your pulse with one hand and run a broadsword up your brisket with the other), described the intellectual and technical rigors of the course of study, pointed out that the other two men in my nursing class were both married and—*sa-lute!*—ex-military, and concluded by stating that the association of this profession with any sort of effete sexual stereotyping was inappropriate, insulting, and inaccurate. As if on cue from Bruce Vilanch, a man in pastel scrubs burst through the door, swept across the room like Isadora Duncan with a stethoscope, clapped his hands à la Corky St. Claire assembling the cast of his latest musical, and lisping like a teakettle, trilled, "Hi everyone! My name is Bob, and I'll be Amy's nurse today!" Nice fella, but he set me back some.

Truth be told, I never suffered for being a male in a female profession. There were small amusements: the same feminist nursing professors who lectured me for referring to my colleagues as "girls" never thought twice about asking me to help lift heavy patients or to strip to my shorts in front of the class for injection demonstrations, and on the day everyone paired up and went behind the curtains to practice breast exams, I got stuck off on a chair in a corner, poking forlornly at a lumpy fake breast.

The only time I ever encountered any gender-based resistance was during my maternity rotation. A woman in the birthing center had agreed to let a student nurse perform her "five point checks," an examination performed in the hours following childbirth to detect any abnormalities or problems. Three of the five points are, to say the least, *specific,* and include a uterus massage.

"Hi," I said, walking into the room. "I'm here to do your five point checks." The woman's eyes widened.

"Who are you?"

"I'm your student nurse."

"Oh. My. God."

I retreated half a step. "If you'd rather . . ."

"I said I didn't mind a student nurse, but I . . ." she trailed off. Then she took a deep breath, rolled her eyes. "Oh, what the hell," she said, hiking her gown. "It's my third kid. Get it over with."

I never did get a little white cap. A few hardcore purists still wear one with defiant pride, but these days classic nursewear is mostly relegated to cheesy porn. I do still have one of my two blue polyester student uniform tops in a box somewhere, but my full-time nursing career was cut short when I dabbled in writing and accidentally made a living. I still have my license, and up until I went on book tour last year, I spent one day a month caring for a neighbor with quadriplegia. In addition to his daily cares, he's on a ventilator and has to have his airway suctioned. It's nothing high-tech, but it keeps me in touch with some of the fundamentals. I'm a little rusty, but if I had to, I could probably put a nasogastric tube up your nose and down your throat (the secret, as I remember, is to have the patient swallow while you thread the needle). I remember how to scrub for surgery (always dry toward your elbows to avoid contaminating your hands). And I know where the suppository goes.

So was it worth it, this male nursing thing? It was and it is. For one thing, nursing has a cyclic history of shortage and surplus, and the current shortage is a doozy. The flier I got in the mail yesterday is typical. It's from a hospital in California. They're offering $23 an hour to nurses fresh out of school. Nurses with eight years' experience are starting at $30 an hour. New nurses get a several-thousand-dollar signing bonus, a $1,000 retention bonus every six months, a fully vested pension plan after six months, and 100 percent paid health insurance. And the hospital pays your moving expenses.

If the economic advantages of a nursing career don't grab you, maybe this will: At school and at work, 90–95 percent of your colleagues will be women. When I graduated from nursing school in 1987, I was one of three males admitted to a class of 92 females. Admission standards were high—these women were intelligent, independent, and professional. And the week we graduated, roughly 15 of them celebrated by ripping the student nurse uniform from my body. To the beat of *Paradise by the Dashboard Light,* no less.

In the end, it's not about boys against girls. Practiced at its best, nursing is humane art. Any good man can do it, and be better for it. The specific job descriptions are limitless: surgical nurse, flight nurse, psychiatric nurse, community health nurse—in short, positions are available all along the continuum of human trouble and existence. Today's nurse is as likely to be working with cutting-edge techno-gadgets as bedpans. This is not your mother's nursing career.

And yet, the thing that invests nursing with its character, with its *power,* is that no matter your field of practice, no matter the technology at your disposal, you will ultimately be providing *care.* My nursing instructors taught me how to start IVs and listen for heart murmurs, but they also taught me to search a patient's eyes, to detect those troubles not audible in the stethoscope tubes or visible on an EKG strip. Employers can up the pay and bennies, I can wink and tell you I still get a little antsy every time I hear Meat Loaf on the oldies station, but the true appeal of nursing lies undeniably in the heart. In an age of violence and irony, what could be more subversive than to *care?*

2011

THE NOT-SO HANDYMAN

The wind is blowing through the front door of the little freestanding building I use as my office. Six months ago the latch went bad. Sometimes when I twisted the handle, nothing would happen. I remedied this by twisting it a lot harder and with deranged vigor, like a hyped-up lab monkey trying to trigger the release of a peanut. I knew this would probably bust the latch in the long term, but for the short term it did the trick. "Don't *ram* on it," my father used to tell us boys when we were using equipment on the farm, but we always did, until the object in question shattered, snapped, or bent—as, eventually, did the latch to my office door. I heard a *crack!* The door handle spun freely, and I found myself effectively locked out.

I should call Terry, I thought. Terry is a legitimate handyman. When the screen door on my porch went bad and my repair attempts made things worse, I hired Terry. When we needed new windows in the house, I hired Terry. *But Terry costs money,* I thought, *and what kind of man can't fix his own door latch?* Using a butter knife, direct blows, and blowtorch curses, I broke in and unscrewed the catch from the door frame so I wouldn't be locked out again, figuring the springs would hold the door closed anyway. Which they did, until a gust of wind sucked the delatched door open, ripping out both springs, badly warping the frame, and cracking the jamb to an extent that now Terry is going to be very expensive indeed.

◆ ◆ ◆

Why is it so tough for so many of us to admit defeat and hire a person to do the job right? I would never dream of doing my own knee replacement, but I happily plunge into projects around the house for which I am equally unqualified. As a wannabe handyman, I'm haunted by high hopes, false starts, and even worse finishes. The evidence surrounds me. The bathroom faucet I bought and never installed. (It's still there, under the sink.) The engine heater I bought and let sit until the packaging fell away. The hole in the doghouse door patched over with a piece of plywood. I did manage to repair a leaky garden hose this summer. Took me three tries, but I did it. Then I left the hose in the driveway and my mother-in-law ran over it. It's leaking again.

Part of the problem is that a man like me ought to be handy. I grew up on a farm. I ran machinery. I used wrenches, hammers, grease guns, and saws. I stacked things and shoveled stuff. I spent five summers working on a ranch in Wyoming, fixing busted sickle sections and making minor repairs to the haymaking equipment. I had grease under my nails and scabs on my knuckles. But even at the peak of my game—even when my hands were heavily callused—I was mostly skating. Anything more complicated than a nut off a bolt or a nail needing a hammer, and I was sunk. And even with those simple tasks, I was easily flummoxed and prone to self-mutilation—a pattern dating back to when I was five years old.

Dad was remodeling the barn, and I decided to help. It was deepest winter, but I bundled up and trekked outside, determined to pitch in. Dad handed me a hammer. The first thing I did was lick it. Instead of the sweet, electric taste of the shiny steel, I felt a numb, crinkly sensation as the hammerhead froze fast to my tongue. Panicking, I yanked it loose, pulling away a perfect circle of skin. I forsook carpentering and went back into the house to read comics and taste the raw spot over and over.

◆ ◆ ◆

I long to be an old-school guy—a guy who can frame things up, tweak a carburetor, break out the soldering iron and fix Junior's toy train. A guy who can fix his own door latch. But time and time again I have proved that I'm not that guy. And so I marvel at the plumber and the way he replaces the sink drain in just one try. I wonder what it's like to be the furnace guy—to hook things up, snap things together, and walk away with no wires dangling and nothing smoking. I'm astounded when Terry hangs a door and it swings shut with a secure click. And it's so much worse when you were raised around capable people with a work ethic. I have that ethic and I want to lend a hand, but I often find people like my brother, a man who regularly tears bulldozers apart and re-assembles them, letting me have a go and then gently taking the wrench from me with a look that says, *Okay, recess is over . . .*

I can build disaster from the simplest repair job. We have a smallish tractor here on the farm, and recently the battery went dead. No problem. I pulled the pickup truck beside it, hooked up the jumper cables, and—instead of revving the engine impatiently ("don't *ram* on it")—went off to multitask while the battery charged. When I returned 10 minutes later, the shed was a haze of toxic smoke, and the battery was fizzing like a junior-high science project.

There are only two ways to hook up a battery, the right way and the wrong way—and the right way is *color coded.* So now I had to replace the battery. I couldn't find the correct wrench (another thing that bugs me about capable people is how organized they are), and the one matching socket I located was stripped. That meant I had to pry the thing out using Vise-Grips and a screwdriver. These are not the proper tools for the job. The cold morning air rang with curses.

I finally wrestled the battery loose and set off to trade it for a new one at the farm store. While I was there, I noticed a bin of cheap wrenches. No self-respecting handyman buys cheap wrenches, so naturally I was interested. The wrench sets were in two bins, but the prices were the same, so I grabbed the nearest set. Back at home, I was almost giddy at the idea of installing the battery now that I had the proper tools. I unrolled the bag of wrenches to select a half-incher, only to find every wrench marked "mm." Two bins of wrenches, and I'd managed to pick the metric ones. The battery bolts (and pretty much everything else on the farm) are standard American. The good news is, you can fling a metric wrench 40 feet, no conversion necessary.

I suspect it's the *feeling* of being a handyman that makes it so tough to drop the hammer and call in a professional. I *enjoy* scuffling beneath a car on a concrete floor. I *like* having nicks on my knuckles. I like puttering, with an old radio playing in the background. I like the secret-clubhouse feeling of being under the sink with just my feet sticking out, same as being under the car with a creeper, the feeling that I'm burrowing in to do good work but also that I'm hiding out under the radar of a high-speed, hectoring world. Then I tighten the drain trap just enough to crack it and the water drips straight into my eye, where it mingles with the tears.

One of our local radio stations airs a program called *Garage Logic*. The show is predicated on the idea that the world's greatest problems can be solved in a garage. The host—a man named Joe—often takes calls from men who say they are "goin' in." In *Garage Logic,* "goin' in" is defined as "making a project so thoroughly and unnecessarily complicated that pretty soon there is no end to it." Like, for instance, attempting to jump-start a tractor but winding up with flying European wrenches, a complete loss of religion, and your own little Superfund site. But as I putter and listen to the show on my battery-operated transistor, what strikes me is that whenever listeners call in to report, "Joe, I'm *goin' in!*" there is absolute joy in their voices. They know it won't end well, and they can't wait to start.

The best thing for a man like me is to have friends who are handy. I have several. One of the best is a guy named Mills, and the other is a guy named Buffalo. When we work together on projects, we enjoy the camaraderie, and I enjoy the idea that I'm pitching in; although when it comes to sweat equity, I'm definitely more sweat than equity. And when it's all over, I get handyman quality for the price of some beers.

I don't always give up. Sometimes I'll finish what I start. And naturally, I take undue pride in those projects I do finish, no matter how cockeyed they end up looking. The slantwise lumber rack out in the garage? The one filled with lumber scraps that are never quite the right length? I built that. The pig waterer that didn't collapse until *after* the pigs had been butchered? Mine. And that crooked chicken coop out there with plastic stapled over where the windows should be? Mine—except for the parts Mills and Buffalo built. Those boys are pretty handy. One day Mills decided to work on the coop without my "help," and in the process of employing his superior skills and equipment, shot himself through the finger with a nail gun. He bled like inbred royalty.

I felt bad for two seconds, and then I asked him if he could fix my office door.

2008

TIM MCGRAW: REAL GOOD BAD EXAMPLE

Sometimes what you need is a real good bad example.

Tim McGraw can name three.

Not counting himself.

Bad example number one would have to be Tug McGraw. Philadelphia Phillies relief pitcher. Threw the final strikeout to win the 1980 World Series. A good-timing quote machine who once said he was unsure if he preferred natural grass to Astroturf because, "I never smoked Astroturf." Did a minor league stint in Florida and left a local high school girl pregnant. "Left" being the operative word, because he blew town and his son Tim would be 11 before he discovered the birth certificate in a closet and learned that superstar in the majors (and, coincidentally, on the baseball card taped to his bedroom wall) was his father. The boy would convince his mom to drive him to the big city ballpark for a meet-up, but Tug wasn't much interested in being Dad, and said as much.

Bad example number two: Horace Smith. Stepfather. Hard worker, good provider, alcoholic. Sweetest, biggest-hearted guy ever, then he'd flip. Beat hell out of the whole damned family. By the time little Tim was in fourth grade, Horace was gone.

Bad example number three: We'll wait on that one.

• • •

"Kale salad!"

The photographer is snapping away, but Tim McGraw just spotted a caterer entering a door clear across the gymnasium-sized studio, and he's hollering for his lunch. The grin on McGraw's face is an acknowledgment of the humor inherent in a country singer calling for kale salad. For now he'll go hungry; that salad is a few hours and a whole lot of photographs down the line.

The soundtrack to the photo shoot, as requested by McGraw's personal assistant, is "classic rock and classic rock, mixed with a little classic rock." The walls reverberate to Rush and the Rolling Stones. Between poses, McGraw joins everyone checking out the raw images on a laptop screen. Sometimes he chuckles, or points and says, "You can paint those wrinkles out, yeah?" But mostly he just moves from pose to pose, clowning one minute, giving you Zoolander Blue Steel (squinty cowboy version) the next. Once he clutches his crotch and jokes he forgot to put the sock in. The photographer has him walk to and fro, and in contrast to his relaxed demeanor, McGraw's gait is bull-rider stiff. His head slides side to side like he's forever trying to peek around a tree, his arms hang gunslinger wide, and wherever he's headed, he leans into it, leading with a pair of deltoids that perch on his shoulders like twin armadillos.

He has no more fat on him than a rope.

"I was looking at some old concert shots the other day," he says, as everyone gathers in for another look. "Man, my *gut!* I was up there in a see-through shirt—I thought I was lookin' *good!*" He turns to his personal assistant. "Why'd you-all let me go onstage like that?"

"You weren't open to conversation about it," she says, raising an eyebrow.

I watch the muscled mega seller stare down the camera from beneath the brim of that famous black hat and I don't think of self-doubt, or uncertainty, but it's there, and always has been. You figure Horace sowed some of that. There was a precarious uncertainty to life with a man who was gentle one minute, violent the next. The young McGraw grabbed that microphone with both hands, but still felt like he could fall.

"Early in my career—I think I was 19—I was so innately shy that to even get up onstage in a club, I'd have to have a few drinks," says McGraw. "I remember my mom tellin' me, 'Y'know if you don't get up there a couple of times without doing that, it's gonna be a problem . . .'"

The clubs became stadiums, the show down the street became life on the road, and as so often happens in life—and country music songs—Mama was right. "I drank too much," says McGraw. "I partied too much. And did other things too much. Chemically. No needles, or that kind of stuff, but . . . use your imagination.

"You're sittin' there on the bus with nothin' to do, and you buy into the whole 'Well, I can't go out, because it'll become a scene' thing, and you get caught in your own little mind. This black trap that you create for yourself."

Now let's talk about bad example number three.

"Keith Whitley—yeah." McGraw shakes his head. "I remember the first time I heard him sing. I had a 1970 Ford pickup. I was up under it, changin' the oil." The place was Start, Louisiana, McGraw's tiny hometown. In fact, you can still hear the bayou in the way he pronounces the word "oil"—*OHL,* drawled thick as used 90-weight.

"I had a radio with batteries in it, and "Miami, My Amy" came on, and I just about knocked my head off, I jumped so much. I turned it up, and thought, *That's* the way it's supposed to be done!"

Whitley was a hard-drinking, death-cheating, lightning-fingered bluegrass phenom out of Kentucky. As brilliant as his playing was, his voice was another gift altogether. "Miami, My Amy" was the first in a volley of singles that would climb the charts. And then, at the age of 34 and right in the middle of a run of number ones, Keith Whitley died—you could say—of his own hand, and in that hand an empty bottle. He would have six more hits, every one of them charting after he was in the grave.

The day Keith Whitley died, Tim McGraw dropped out of college and headed for Nashville.

The photo shoot moves outside. The idea is to capture the back-lot tour workouts that have transformed McGraw from puffy partier to cut teetotaler. A frigid wind sweeps the asphalt. McGraw is wearing nothing but cutoff sweat pants, and even without old photos for comparison, his physique is startling. Ain't no room in that belly for a beer, and if you drove a pickup truck up those abs you'd need new shocks by the time you crossed those pecs, currently chicken-skinning in the cold. McGraw laughs, and points at his nipples.

"Diamond cutters!"

The photographer puts McGraw through his paces: Alternating arm waves on the battle ropes, high-box step-ups, core-building twists with the heavy chains. Soon he's warm despite the wind. "I'll be the first to admit I take it to extremes," says the singer, after knocking out a set of plyometric push-ups (McGraw calls them "Spidermans") that had him springing clear of the ground. "I'm not one of those people who can sorta half-ass something."

A man that maniacal about his abs, you can only imagine how he obsesses over his million-dollar throat. Until you ask, and he laughs. "It's not like polishin' silver. I'm not Pavarotti. My voice training comes with two hours of shows every night. I mean, I can warm up all I want—I don't—and it's not gonna make a hill'a beans difference.

"I'm a storyteller, not a singer."
Keith Whitley, now, *he* was a singer.
And a damn good bad example.

"Keith Whitley taught me how demons can overtake you if you let 'em," says McGraw. "And I was headed down that path. You let doubt creep into your life. You let uncertainty show its face. You feel like you're supposed to be 'on' all the time. Then you drink and get onstage and all of a sudden you feel confident and powerful. It becomes a habit. Up until seven years ago, there's not a lot of shows I did that I didn't have something in my system."

McGraw won't point to any woke-up-behind-the-dumpster moment that got him to drop the bottle and grab the barbells. He claims four far better reasons: His wife, country singing legend Faith Hill, and their three daughters. "When your wife tells you it's gone too far, that's a big wake-up call. That, and realizing you're gonna lose everything you have. Not monetarily, not career-wise, but family-wise. It got to the point where my kids were getting older, and it was way past the point that they noticed it. And I noticed that they noticed.

"That's enough to straighten you out."

He ponders that a moment. Lets it sink in. Then you see a grin forming. "On a purely egotistical note," says McGraw, who has appeared in several films, "I was in the movie theater and saw a preview of *Four Christmases,* and I saw my big fat face pop up on a hundred-foot screen, and I thought . . . either the bullshit has to go, the confidence has to go, or *somethin'* has to go."

Just prior to our interview, McGraw and Faith Hill concluded an extended run at the Venetian in Las Vegas, appearing together onstage in a relaxed setting to sing and talk. One night McGraw sang the Keith Whitley heartbreaker "Don't Close Your Eyes." Later, in the elevator offstage, he was quiet, and Faith asked him what he was thinking about.

"I just wonder," said McGraw, "what kind of music could we have been hearing from Keith Whitley right now? What would his evolution have been as a singer and songwriter?

"It's sad. Really sad."

Backstage at some summer festival in the early 1990s, I interviewed a young country music singer. He wore a horseshoe mustache and a mullet. Said he was just hoping for a hit so he wouldn't have to go back to pushing a wheelbarrow. A year or so later I saw him again. This time he was descending a brushed aluminum staircase through purple fog beneath a spinning disco ball the size of a Volkswagen Beetle while singing, *"We're just country boys and girls gettin' down on the farm."* As 30,000 people rose to their feet and roared for the new Tim McGraw, I remember thinking, *Well, things change.*

Country music fans aren't always good with that. From his breakout hit ("Indian Outlaw," which landed him in hot cultural water) right up to his recent single, the overtly Auto-Tuned "Lookin' for That Girl," McGraw has long incurred criticism for pushing some boundaries while hewing too closely to others. But for every good-time party number like "I Like It, I Love It," and "Truck Yeah," derided by critics in terms of fluff and Velveeta, McGraw delivers a "Red Ragtop" (about young lovers and abortion) or the recent "Highway Don't Care."

McGraw's reaction? Well, he told you before: He's a story-teller, not a singer. "There are people who will never have a shot at a career but can sing circles around me. I know that. But the people I gravitate to as an artist, and the people I like to listen to, are people I *believe.* You don't have to have lived every song you sing. It's not about that. It's about conveying a sense of honesty. Or finding a place within you that can relate to that and empathize with the character in the song."

You think he can't do it? You think he's all "Mexicoma," or "Refried Dreams"? Hunt down the songs "Drugs or Jesus," or "Walk

Like a Man." Have a listen, and imagine a little boy wondering which Horace Smith was going to come through the door that night. Imagine that same boy, a little older now, sneaking out of bed to watch from the top stair step as his single mother weeps over a coffee table covered in unpayable bills even though the boy now knows his biological father is a ball-playing millionaire. Now close your eyes, and listen again. You'll hear an artist conveying vulnerability from a place not available via Auto-Tune.

Horace White, the second bad example, set one good example. "One of the things I learned from my stepdad was a really strong work ethic," says McGraw. "He was a trucker, he was a cowboy, he was a farmer, he did all sorts of things, but he always showed up for work. He always got the job done."

So if a stadium full of fans want to hear "Refried Dreams," one more time, you don't go all agonizing artist, you go out there and get the job done. No matter what sort of offstage trouble might be percolating.

And there's where the parallel ends. Because the stepson quit the bad habits before the family quit him. But as he flips into a set of handstand pushups against the front of a gleaming black tour bus, you'll note he whipped the whiskey with workouts. Even in that, there was a little nod to Horace and the idea of showing up.

"This is probably not as healthy as I think."

It's late afternoon. The shoot is done, and McGraw is answering my questions around mouthfuls of that long-awaited kale salad. "It's got cranberries, and Parmesan cheese . . . but it makes me *feel* good!"

Summer is coming. Within weeks of this interview McGraw will be trading the crystal chandeliers of Vegas for the dust and mud of the festival circuit, and that's just fine. "It takes me back to when I was a kid. We'd go to these Fourth of July things down on the Ouachita River, and everybody's crowded around and the fireworks are goin' off . . . It's a great way to enjoy country music, and it's just so *American*."

Late in the game, Tug and Tim had their time together. Tug hung out on the tour bus, Tim got to know his stepsister and stepbrother. It wasn't one long Hallmark moment. Tim has been known to say there were times he felt more like the father than the son. But when Tug found himself dying of brain cancer, Tim and Faith were part of the circle who drew around him. He died at their farm.

"There's still some days when I wake up thinking, 'I hate that son-of-a-bitch,'" says McGraw. "There's a weight that comes from growing up in that sort of situation and sometimes it's suffocating. But when I found out Tug was my dad, I felt like I could break the surface and breathe. It gave me a drive and a confidence to try to do something with my life."

And then there was the more prosaic fact: Tim McGraw's first record deal? It came about after the friend of a record executive heard Tim's audition tape while hitching a ride with—Tug McGraw. If Tug did the right thing late in the game, well, that was his thing.

It's tempting to put a ribbon on it. Be satisfied with the conceit of bad examples yielding good. Ignore the fact that the bottle never stops calling. That the hits won't always keep coming. That Tim McGraw's mom delivered him, through it all and in every sense. That she is his foundation.

So we'll stop with the art of conjecture and leave you with a solid fact: Tim McGraw, doing his job, his own best bad example, living right and stabbing that kale salad.

2014

NEW YEAR'S RESOLUTION:
MEET MILLS AT THE WIDOWMAKER

My editor at Men's Health Magazine *asked me to contribute a short piece about New Year's resolutions. I don't make them, but I wrote this anyway because A) self-employment, and B) I was hoping it would be so.*

In an ideal 2007 I would spend more time at the Widowmaker with my pal Mills—the funniest man ever to don a set of plastic hillbilly teeth. I think "The Widowmaker" would be a great name for a strip club, but our Widowmaker is simply a big dead tree, felled by a beaver so that the trunk lies parallel to a secret channel running between the Chippewa River and a backwater slough. When the river rises, the channel reverses flow, drawing in schools of foraging carp. We stand on the horizontal tree trunk with our bows and arrows and try to snipe the carp as they cruise past. For pickup truck boys like me and Mills, carp shooting is the dream pastime: fishing and hunting, combined.

Mills first took me to the Widowmaker in the late 1990s. Before long I was sneaking off to shoot carp the way some guys sneak off to happy hour. I am self-employed and should have been working; instead I'd be at my computer and on the phone with Mills as we both studied our screens, scanning animated North Central US Infrared Satellite feeds, assessing emerging cloud patterns. If you want to shoot carp, you've got to have clear, sunny skies, and the minute it looked like the clouds were bound to part above the Widowmaker, we were on our way, driving from opposite ends of the county to meet beneath a graffiti-sprayed overpass, where we followed a half-hidden footpath through the poison ivy to the river-bank, climbed atop the log, and commenced to firing. One time Mills got there before me, and when I walked up behind him he turned—dressed head to toe in camo—and grinned widely, reveal-ing those fake Bubba choppers. They jutted from his mouth like a batch of rejected Chiclets. We laughed so hard he spit the teeth.

Last year, Mills and I made it to the Widowmaker exactly once. We saw a single shadowy carp, and didn't fire a shot. I wish I could say 2006 was an anomaly, but in fact, it is the end of a sharp taper. In 2002, after years of self-employed scrabbling, the jobs came pouring in. Things got busy. Things got shuffled off the schedule.

Carp shooting, for one. Mills, for another.

I do not care for the term "best friend." It's too brittle. The nature of friendships varies based on past performance and current needs. Sometimes it comes down to proximity, or a shared affin-ity for shooting fish. Friendships shift and adjust along with the rest of your life. And sometimes, when things get busy, you put your most loyal friends on hold. You trust them to understand, and they do. But lately I am thinking there must be a limit. One of my good pals just had his heart broken by his live-in of eight years, and I've been tending to him mostly by cell phone, which is a ridiculous substitute for a smoky bar. Another friend just left rehab, and I was reduced to sending my best wishes from the road. Selfishly, perhaps, I am thinking I am the one being cheated here. It isn't that I need to bless my friends with my presence; it's that I need to bless myself with *their* presence.

I can feel the Chippewa River out there beneath the ice, mov-ing day and night, just one more clock running down. It is time I attended to my friends. Let it begin now, in the dead of winter, when I flip the calendar to May and block off a few days for Mills. For the Widowmaker. For the marauding carp of Chippewa County.

2007

P.S. Every year we still block off a few days. A decade now and we've only made it back out once. But just last night Mills and I were needling each other via text message. When he needed me to speak at a funeral on his behalf a while ago, I did it. When he needed a 25-ton hydraulic wood splitter, I lent him mine, and he towed it home behind his motorcycle, perhaps wearing those hillbilly teeth. When I needed secondhand firefighting gear for a play I was putting on, he rounded it up. When I needed a meat grinder to make venison sausage, he lent me his. The friendship shifts, adjusts, and sustains.

MUSKY HUNTING

Jim Saric needs to catch a musky. The fish is out there some-where, torpedo-smooth and moody beneath 40,000 acres of slate-gray chop, a prehistoric-style killing machine working the shoreline on a slow, malevolent cruise, sometimes stopping to suspend sniper-still in the murk. The fish knows it can whip any-thing in the pond and will not be hurried. A musky (muskie in some regions—both short for *muskellunge*) does not bite until it's good and ready. This makes it tough to catch. "Fish of 10,000 casts," the old-timers call it.

And *bite* doesn't quite cover it. A musky operates with over-whelming force. Trimmed out like a subaquatic Phantom jet, it leads with a flat snout nestled into a protrusive mandible. As the largest member of the pike family, the fish looks perpetually truculent. When kill time comes, its mandible gapes, unsheath-ing a jawful of gatory shivs, perfect for the initial smash-and-grab. In contrast, the roof of the mouth is a twisted thicket of suture-needle teeth, all angled backward to keep the victim gullet-bound. A musky does not bite. It engulfs, clamps, and then chokes its meal down whole. It has been known to eat ducks, muskrats, and—so they say at the tavern—the occasional dog-paddling poodle.

Jim Saric needs to catch a musky because he is the host and executive producer of the *Musky Hunter* television show. He's been fighting the wind and waves here on northern Minnesota's Lake Vermilion for two days. He's already landed two muskies for the camera, but he needs one more to fill the third and final spot between commercials. Over the past 25 years, Saric has boated more than 140 muskies exceeding 50 inches in length—the largest weighing 53 pounds. He has won seven professional musky-fishing tournaments. He's also the editor of *Musky Hunter* magazine and co-author of *The Complete Guide to Musky Fishing*. He has produced training videos including *Musky Hunter Tactics, Muskies at the Next Level,* and *Precision Musky Presentations.* He has numerous corporate sponsors, a $60,000 powerboat loaded with the latest full-color digital gadgets, and—in case you're thinking "Bubba"—a master's degree in hydrogeology.

He will bring all these things to bear to catch that final fish.

And then he will let it go.

When I was a kid in the country, we caught panfish for dinner, bass for kicks, and carp for no good reason. We sat on docks and flipped worms at lily pads in the sun. But when talk turned to muskies, we pulled our toes from the water and spoke reverentially of the handful of locals we knew who had caught one. The road past my family's farm led to a lake known for muskies, and every evening around suppertime, a man named Charles Hanson would shoot past in his pickup, boat in tow, bound to hook one. He made that trip regularly for 16 years before he caught his first. "November 10, 1968!" he says. You wonder if he can rattle off his wedding anniversary as readily.

Hanson and several pals started a musky-conservation group and began stocking and creating musky habitat in local lakes. Today, thanks to people like him, the musky population is thriving. "Musky anglers have definitely been leaders in fishery conservation," says Tim Simonson, a fisheries biologist with the Wisconsin Department of Natural Resources Bureau of Fisheries Management. "Voluntary release of muskellunge has grown steadily since the early 1970s, to the point where many avid musky anglers now release every fish they catch." Of the 200,000 or so muskies now caught annually in Wisconsin, all but around 5,000 were returned to the water. (Legally, a musky must be at least 34 inches long to keep.) Quite a switch from the early days. "We used to shoot muskies," Hanson says ruefully. "My buddy had a .38 auto mounted on a .45 frame. You didn't even have to hit 'em to kill 'em . . . just come close!"

Nowadays the fish are found in 37 states, up from 24 in 1978. "Minnesota is probably the greatest success story," says Saric. "Twenty years ago, half the current musky fisheries didn't exist." He also cites Colorado, Utah, and Washington as states where the fish is gaining ground, and says that musky fishing in Canada is "awesome." The bottom line, according to Saric: "This is no longer the fish of 10,000 casts."

"It's now the fish of 3,000 casts," agrees Patricia Strutz, a musky hunter who owns a guiding service in northern Wisconsin. "But that's still a lot of casts!"

What, then, compels hordes of freshwater Ahabs to froth the waters so? Strutz credits the musky's twin auras of menace and indifference. "They eat when they want to eat," she says. "To have a huge fish follow your lure and then turn away . . ." And when the tension does break, it breaks huge. "Muskies fight more like saltwater big game," says Strutz. "They jump completely out of the water, dance across the surface on their tails, thrash wildly, and dive beneath the boat."

More than one angler has taken hooks to the face when a musky has risen from the depths, rattled its bony gills, and spit the lure straight back at the boat. "Salmon fight harder," says Richard Minich, author of *Becoming a Musky Hunter,* "and smallmouth bass are more exciting pound for pound. But who's afraid of a salmon or a smallie? If there's a chance to go fishing generally, I might go. If there's a chance to go fishing for muskies, I go."

"Musky fever is a true addiction," says Strutz. "I've seen grown men shake violently, mumble for 10 minutes incoherently, and even cry when they lose a big one."

I caught a musky once—accidentally. I was young and it was

tiny. I released it and failed to contract musky fever. I wonder if I'm immune?

"Step into my office!" Saric booms, ushering me off the dock and into his 20-foot 620VS Ranger Fisherman. We're joined by his cameraman, Jim Lucy, and Dick Heckel, who's fishing as Saric's guest. Saric fires the 250-horse Mercury outboard and we roar across the lake to our first stop. Selecting a large bucktail lure—a spinner and hooks dressed with a wad of tinsel—Saric addresses the camera to record one of the many talking points he'll later splice into the show.

"Right now we're fishing yesterday's wind," he says, explaining that early-morning muskies are still patterned on the previous day's weather conditions. A slim, brown-haired man with a direct gaze and matter-of-fact tone, he has a knack for breaking things down.

Saric works his reel hard, horsing the bait back through the water at a steady crank. The rod he's using is fairly flexible and between seven and a half and eight and a half feet long—the combination allows for longer casts and better control—and threaded with a fine, no-stretch braided line capable of holding 80 pounds before breaking. When the lure is six feet from the boat, he dips the rod tip, driving it underwater to stir a figure eight in the water. Muskies are notoriously finicky, more famous for following the bait than taking it. But they can be provoked. The figure eight is a tease intended to trip some primordial neural trigger. Saric estimates that it generates 20 percent of all strikes.

Just as things settle into a groove, Saric says "Next!" and fires up the boat to send us roaring back across the lake. A red line on a dash-mounted LCD traces our progress in real time. The display is linked to a sonar unit containing a map chip tied into a GPS system. Saric can view the underwater topography in three-foot slices and place navigational icons on the screen. When he catches a musky, he'll log the coordinates, length of the fish, lure, weather conditions, wind direction, temperature, time of day, and moon phase. "Muskies are triggered by environmental factors," Saric says. "I'm trying to figure out what fish do over time. Not just *where* I can catch them but *when.*" Two of Saric's favorite triggers are sunset and moonrise. "They create a 15-minute window of strong feeding," he says. "We know they're going to bite before they know they're going to bite."

We glide to a stop along a new stretch of shoreline. Each time the lures hit the water, a puff of spray hangs in the sunlight. "Next!" yells Saric, and we cut another red line across the sonar screen.

We fish for several hours, buzzing all over the lake. The lures go out, the lures come in. There is the whistle of the unspooling line, the muted grind of the reel, the thump of waves on the hull, the rocking of the boat. "The water's warming up," Saric says at one point. "It was 61.9 degrees; now it's 63.8." The temperature rise can spike a musky's metabolism, which sometimes is all it takes to trip the switch. The conversation ebbs and flows as we watch the water for that swirl, that roll of a slimy back, that flash of a white maw. After so many fruitless retrieves, it's hard to visualize the eruption, but that's what we're in for should the musky decide to get with the script. All morning, Saric and Heckel have been telling musky stories, and not once have I heard the word *bite.* "They *eat* those topwater lures!" "That fish just *blew up* the bait!" "He *T-boned* it!" "He *crushed* it!" The air is filled with exclamation points. Not so the water.

"Next!"

The largest musky in the world is 145 feet long and dominates the grounds of the Freshwater Fishing Hall of Fame, in Hayward, Wisconsin. Entering near the anus, visitors climb the innards of the fish and emerge in the mouth, four and a half stories above the ground. Sometimes people get married between the teeth. Wisconsin, and Hayward in particular, has long been the epicenter of musky fishing in America. The three top world-record muskies were taken in Wisconsin, and two of those were pulled from the Chippewa Flowage, a 15,300-acre tangle of water and wilderness formed by the installation of a dam in 1923, just outside Hayward. The current record fish—69 pounds 11 ounces and 63.5 inches long—was caught in the Flowage by Hayward local Louie Spray in 1949. Louie lost the crown in 1957 when a New Yorker fishing the St. Lawrence River caught a musky weighing 69 pounds 15 ounces.

However, the Hall of Fame deposed the New York fish in 1992 after analyzing a photograph in which it appeared much smaller than claimed. Not coincidentally, a vocal contingent of the musky world believes Louie Spray's fish is also fraudulent. Among other things, they point out that the man who initiated the disqualification of the New York fish owns a resort on the lake where Louie caught his, and also that he has written a book about Louie's exploits.

Piscatory conspiracy theorists have a lot to chew on. An adversarial report filed by the World Record Musky Alliance (WRMA) features 49 pages of sworn statements, affidavits, diagrams, expert photo analysis, legal opinions, comments from a Canadian crime-scene investigator, and a profusion of professionally worded aspersions culminating in the accusation that the Hall of Fame is covering for its hometown boy. In 2006, it rejected the WRMA report and reconfirmed Louie's record.

There is much at stake. A replica of Louie's musky—the original was lost in a fire—is on display at the Hall of Fame, and the Flowage's reputation attracts customers for area guides, who can charge up to $350 a day. The Wisconsin Department of Natural Resources estimates that musky anglers spend $425 million in the state annually. The average *Musky Hunter* reader spends nearly $3,500 a year on the pursuit, and that's not including the purchase of boats, motors, and trailers.

When I ask Saric about the controversy, he remains politic but says he fears musky fishing will become like boxing, with different sanctioning bodies keeping different records and anointing different champions. There is only one way to resolve the Hall of Fame dispute: Somebody has to catch a 70-pounder.

By late afternoon the water is busting the sun into a million little twinkles. Still no fish. Saric ties on a lure the size of a squirrel. It's made of fluorescent orange rubber and wiggles through the water like an overgrown salamander. "Sometimes, when things are slow, you have to use a 'shocker' bait to rouse the fish," he says. Not to catch them, he explains, just to raise them.

Heckel has turned to throwing a topwater bait, a buoyant, torpedo-shaped plug trimmed with a silver propeller that spins half in and half out of the water, leaving a trail of tiny bubbles. We're working a small island surrounded by large rocks, many of them barely submerged. It's quiet again. Not much talking. Just the tinny jingle of the propeller blades and the rattle of the treble hooks when a lure is flying, followed by the burbly putt-putt of its return.

"There's one!" I yell. I've been doing my level best to remain the silent observer, but when a big fish rolls just behind and below Heckel's lure, I blurt without reservation. The image stuck to my retina is of a gray-green curve—no head, no tail, just the flank of the fish curling back on itself. Suddenly the day is galvanized. Heckel saw the fish, too, and he's nearly dancing. He flings his bait again. Nothing. But Saric wants to keep working the spot. "The idea that muskies are a 'loner fish' is a myth," he says. "Five, six, seven muskies in the same spot is common. It's like a wolf pack. Maybe you'll get one real big one on its own, but generally they hang out together." After a few more fruitless passes, we move on.

But something has changed. Saric and Heckel both raise muskies on several of our next stops. They don't bite; they just slide behind the lure or—and this puts a catch in your breath—rise into view right beside the boat. Saric isn't worried that they're not hitting. "On a nice, bright day, you'll get a lot of lookers. That doesn't mean you won't get one to come and eat, but the conditions have to be right." He's happy we're seeing these fish. He knows they're there. And when the conditions are right, he'll be back.

For the next two hours, though, the action stops. Then we rework a stretch of shoreline where a fish followed earlier in the day, and Heckel is hollering again. "There's one! There's one!" He figure-eights like mad. "Take a longer sweep!" Saric commands. Heckel extends his stroke, and suddenly there's an explosion. "I got 'im!" Heckel yells. Saric is barking instructions and scrambling for the net. "Bring him around the front! Drive his head down! Drive his head down!"

And then the thing is netted and in the boat. It's a python-bellied lunker. "Whoo!" says Heckel. "Whooooo!"

Moving quickly, Saric measures the fish. Forty-nine inches. Nowhere near a record, but a fine musky nonetheless. Facing the camera, Saric congratulates Heckel and works in a seamless talking point about the importance of returning to spots where you've had follows. Then he looks directly at the lens and says, "Join us next week on a big fish adventure on . . . *The Musky Hunter!*" And then the fish is back in the water and we roar off to the next spot. The sun sinks; Saric and Heckel continue to fish. On the horizon, the red lights of a faraway radio tower pulse slowly and ever brighter in the sky. When the rods are finally stowed, night is fully upon us. The horsepower thunders us home and the sonar glows against Saric's face as we cut a final red line through the crisscross day.

There are less intensive approaches to catching muskies. "I fish out of a 70-year-old boat," says musky guide and row-trolling advocate Dave Schnell. Rather than roar around flinging lures, Schnell and his clients use oar power and mostly trail their lures behind the boat. "Row trolling is quiet, great exercise, and you get a real sense of accomplishment when you row for five hours and then hook into a big fish," Schnell says.

Somewhere between the extremes of Saric and Schnell, you find musky hunters like my old neighbor Charles Hanson. A week after my outing with Saric, Hanson and I push away from the dock of a small lake in Chippewa County, Wisconsin. The boat is small and there is very little gear—not even a depth finder. "On large lakes you fish spots," he says. "Here we can fish the whole lake."

Hanson, whose curly hair turned white long ago, is fishing a bucktail specially constructed to slip through weeds without snagging. He designed the lure himself, but as he points to a tackle box jammed with lures of every concoction, he says, "There's nothing new under the sun . . . everything's a variation on a theme." His take on all the doodads available to today's musky hunter is equally dismissive. "I used to study solar tables, lunar tables, subscribe to all the magazines, learn all the theories. Now my theory is that the best time to go musky fishing is whenever you can make it!"

For three hours we just drift, fish, and talk. With no TV show to fill, the pressure's off. Finally, Charles looks at the sky, overcast and spitting rain. "Let's fish that first stretch one more time," he says, pointing to the shoreline where we began the day.

It's not the wildest spot on earth: pine trees and brush broken by lake-house lawns and the few docks that haven't been pulled for the season. A few short weeks ago the water was flotsammed with vacationers. Now they're mostly gone, and the only signs of life come from two guys grinding a tree stump.

I was asleep at the switch on the first follow and went to the figure eight way too slowly. A swab of green-gray and then the musky was gone. Forty yards down the shoreline, I have another follow. I figure-eight immediately, but again the fish demurs. Then I hear an exclamation from Charles—the musky is now snapping at his figure eight.

And then nothing. Somehow it missed the hooks. We cover another 40 yards of shore, but nothing happens. Casting toward a boat lift, I misjudge the distance and brake the reel harshly to prevent the lure from clanking into the cross-members. The line jerks and the bait drops clumsily, a vertical knuckleball nearly clipping the dock. It ain't pretty, but I take only two cranks before I feel an electric *b-bump-bump-TUG* coming up through the line. Like a kid, I yelp, "There he is!"

"Set the hook!" says Charles, and I horse the rod once, twice, like I'm pitching forkfuls of cow manure over my shoulder, and then I focus on getting the fish to the boat. Charles is ready with the net, but just when the musky looks as if it's pointed in the right direction, it takes off around the front of the boat and I can hear Saric's voice in my head: "Drive his head down! Drive his head down!" I jam the rod tip into the water, half guiding and half following the fish in as it semicircles the bow. I get my first good look at it now, and the best I can muster is, "Shnikies!"

And then it's in the net. Charles is grinning ear to ear, and me the same. Just goofy with the thrill of it all. When I hold the fish up for a pre-release picture, I can smell it, murky and fresh in the same whiff. It measures 33 inches—nowhere near the legal length—but as it courses away from the boat to fight another day, it is a good place to be: this lake, this boat, this gray musky day.

2009

P.S. By the time this piece was published, Charles Hanson was dying. When I visited him in the hospital he couldn't speak, but his eyes lit up as we relived "our gray musky day." From my writing desk I can see the Polaroid he took in the boat. That fish was nearly a yard long; my smile is equivalently wide.

WHY MEN GET A BANG OUT OF GUNS

You might not suspect it if you see me flat-footing down the sidewalk in my rumpled duds, but I am legally authorized to carry concealed upon my person a handgun, a stun gun, a billy club, and various knives.

If you're looking for an NRA sticker on my truck window, you won't find one.

If you're looking for my underground bunker, you won't find one.

If you're looking for my stockpile of ammo and weapons, you won't find one—at least not one that will last beyond the first wave of zombies, or several deer-hunting seasons.

And frankly, if you're looking for my concealed weapon, you probably won't find one.

But I have reserved the option.

We can all recite (or screech) the cases for and against gun control. I have nothing to add in either respect, at least nothing that will look punchy on a placard or nifty on a T-shirt. I'm pro-gun the way I'm pro–potato fork. I use both to gather food for the year, with the caveat that if you break into my house, I won't be waiting at the top of the stairs with a potato fork.

Actually, I can't even live up to the braggadocio of what I just wrote, but more on that shortly. After years of political tussling, my home state of Wisconsin now grants properly permitted citizens the right to carry a concealed weapon. Back when the fight was at its fever pitch, I took to the habit of saying that the only thing I found less compelling than the arguments for conceal/ carry were the arguments against it. I also said that if the law ever passed, I'd apply for a permit on the simple grounds that I might as well avail myself of all options.

But why? What motivates guys like me—who live in a relatively safe area and are neither running scared nor itching for a fight—to even consider traveling armed at all times? In a 2012 study from the University of Texas at Austin, sociologist Angela Stroud, PhD, put the question to men who possessed concealed carry permits, and the answers fell into three categories: "(1) to protect their wives and children from violent crime; (2) to compensate for lost physical strength as they age; and (3) to make them feel more secure in places they feel vulnerable."

Regarding reason 2, I'm not the man I used to be, but I was never really Rambo in the first place, so I'm not sure it applies. But the other two reasons have some traction and may be part of the reason why, one evening, I went online and printed my concealed-weapon application. It was a simple form including instructions to supply "proof of training" followed by a long list of acceptable options. First was "hunter education program." Toggling over to the state Department of Natural Resources site, I brought up my file, and there it was: my hunter's safety certificate, completed back in 1977—when I was 13 years old. I slipped a copy into an envelope along with a scan of my driver's license and a check for 50 bucks, walked to the end of the driveway, dropped the packet into the mailbox, and raised the red flag.

Seven days later I opened the mailbox again, and there it was: my license to carry a concealed weapon in Wisconsin.

My father forbade me and my brothers to possess toy guns or to pretend to shoot each other with our fingers. He also raised us in a religious sect that banned movies and television, so we were hardly immersed in the dreaded "culture of violence." And yet whenever I visited friends, we dove straight for the plastic pistols and went full-on O.K. Corral. Even before I took to reading war stories and cowboy books in third grade, I was so desperate to have a toy rifle that I cobbled one together from a yardstick and part of a drawing easel and proudly showed it to a friend on the kindergarten school bus.

I first squeezed the trigger of a real gun sometime around the age of 9 or 10. My father's arms were around me, steadying my aim. According to some experts, his presence then shaped my feelings about firearms now. "That's an emotional connection that is often left out of the conversation," says Stroud. "One thing that stuck out in my interviews was how deeply meaningful guns can become for boys who have these experiences with their fathers. I think a lot of anti-gun people don't really understand gun culture and what it means to grow up in a place where young boys—more than girls—have guns and hunting as a part of a family experience. They have positive associations with using guns and with being out shooting."

Sure enough, I remember how eagerly I would look forward to those times when Dad would cut out of work to set up a line of pop cans on a log for us to "plink." My father was a quiet man who drilled me on safety and had no patience for swagger, but at some level I saw his willingness to take me shooting as a prelude to manhood. "You were learning what it means to be a man, and you still want to advertise that fact," says Frank McAndrew, PhD, a psychology professor at Knox College in Illinois who researches human social behavior. "Especially if you grew up in a rural area, guns are part of that image. Just like having a pickup truck or any of the other trappings of manhood. So if you're walking around without a gun, somehow you're not complete. It's kind of like if you were forced to drive a Volkswagen Beetle instead of a pickup truck. It's emasculating."

What McAndrew doesn't know is that I own two pickup trucks.

Also a Volkswagen Jetta.

Maybe I'd better get a bigger gun.

You might not know from all the fear-fueled in-your-face "man card" bluster, but there are legions of us out here who have guns and have always had guns, and we attach to this all the dramatic significance of having silverware. Once when I was standing beside my brother John at his sawmill, our fire department pagers went off and called us to stand by with the county SWAT team. "We have a report of a man holed up in his house with a gun," said the dispatcher. John looked at me quizzically. "Hmmm . . ." he said. "That's me every night!"

Today I own three rifles, one shotgun, and one revolver. This is likely low-average for my geographic peer group and *way* low for my immediate family, and it leaves me in Ted Nugent's dust along with all the rest of you. I'm hardly a gun nut, not even in the hobbyist sense. I can't rattle off ballistics or model numbers or muzzle velocities. I can break down and reassemble my firearms for cleaning, but if I dismantle trigger mechanisms, springs might start flying.

That said, I do a modest amount of target shooting every year to keep in trim between hunting seasons, and I recently joined the rest of the family in firing my brother-in-law's AR-15 during a get-together. When my brother John and I were young, we would shake up beer cans and then shoot them, reveling in the foamy explosion.

"Men love guns for all kinds of different reasons," says McAndrew. "The mere act of handling and firing a gun is biologically rewarded. We get a testosterone rush. That's pleasant. It's the same as when you win a tennis match, or achieve something at work where you won out in a competition against a guy for a job. Your adrenaline levels go up."

To verify this, McAndrew and his colleagues checked the testosterone levels of 30 male college students before and after the students played with either a gun or a children's game for 15 minutes. The men who'd played with the gun had significantly higher readings. And that, McAndrew says, boils down to one conclusion: "Shooting guns is fun."

But what made it fun to pull the trigger in the first place? Perhaps it began, as so many quirks of human behavior begin, with evolution.

In a 2010 study review, David Puts, PhD, a researcher at Penn State, concluded that the manufacture and use of weapons probably helped our knuckle-dragging male ancestors score the best dates and even "monopolize multiple females." Puts cites research postulating that evolving females consciously selected those men who were best equipped to provide protection from rape and to shield offspring from harm, but he doubts many women will be interested in a man simply because he's packing a big pistol. "Happily," says Puts, "times have changed." Sometimes a gun is just a gun.

We live at the terminus of a dead-end country road. Crime in this area is very low, but I have more than once returned home after midnight to find strange cars parked at the turnaround. When I beamed them with the headlights, they took off. Who knows? Could've been some kids necking and drinking, or could've been someone casing my place.

Even with a few friends in the sheriff's department, I have no guarantee that anyone will be able to arrive in time should I, or my wife and daughters, call for help. So it does not seem all that unreasonable that I keep a 12-gauge shotgun at hand in the bedroom—although that gun is pretty long and was not designed for working in tight spaces.

The one time I ever took up arms against an intruding human was when I was roused from sleep at 3 a.m. by the sound of someone rattling the side door to my garage. I grabbed the shotgun from beside my bed, rolled off the mattress, and quickly made my way to the screen window that overlooks the space between the house and the garage. I got there just in time to catch a glimpse of two figures entering and pulling the door shut behind them.

I could hear every word they said, and in a matter of minutes it became clear to me that these were not top-flight theft ninjas: They were looking to steal gasoline and, lacking flashlights, were searching for the unleaded using their cigarette lighters.

When I'd been entertained long enough, I stood with my shotgun at the ready and hollered, "You boys better HIT THE ROAD!"

After some drunken back-and-forth between themselves, the two men departed.

I leaned the shotgun against the wall and went back to bed. In the morning I realized that I had completely forgotten to remove the trigger lock. Basically I was standing there with a 12-gauge baseball bat.

According to his website, Dan Marcon is a corrections officer with a degree in police science who served five years in the military and worked for a private security firm. According to me, he is the walking, well-armed personification of the phrase "brick shithouse." We met when I took his Wisconsin/Non-Resident CCW class that—via some baroque interstate "reciprocity" arrangements—will expand my concealed carry rights to as many as 35 states.

I enjoyed the class. Marcon knows his stuff and is an energetic instructor. When I asked him why people enroll, he said, "They want it for protection, because society is going south fast. The violence—the everyday violence in towns that never really had violence, where people weren't locking their doors, like the area where we're from [Marcon and I grew up near each other], now they have to lock their doors. One worry is the influx of people who have no jobs, who are on drugs or under the influence of narcotics, people who find the easy road to take from someone who has." When Marcon really gets going, he'll tell you that Hitler got his start by taking guns away.

That isn't my perception of the current situation, and that isn't my reading of history. But then again, I once listened to a PhD type equate John Ashcroft to Himmler and Goebbels. Then, in the time it took to refresh her wine and cheese, she informed me that I shouldn't fear registering my guns with John Ashcroft's government.

We're all afraid of something. I have no illusions about the violence real guns can do, and the price we pay for their pervasiveness. While working as an EMT, I once cared for two gunshot victims in one day. The first was a police officer who had responded to a domestic complaint and was shot by an assailant. We did everything we could, and then I held his hand as we raced for the hospital. He squeezed my fingers to let me know he could hear me. Just as we turned him over to the surgeons, we were paged back to the scene to pick up the shooter, who had subsequently blown off one side of his own skull. He died in the back of the ambulance. The physician who came out to the ambulance bay to make the call told us the officer had died in surgery.

This single incident hardly qualifies me as a combat-hardened vet, but I carry vivid visions of those wounds in my memory, and even more the sense of irretrievable finality wrought by gunshots. Several years later I was called to provide medical support to a SWAT-style emergency-response team as it took down an active shooter. I remember the adrenaline surging as I hunkered with two other EMTs in the front of the ambulance waiting for the "go" command. Suddenly a shot rang out. I responded by ducking my head and hollering, *"Fuck!"*

In short, I ain't looking for a fight.

Transitioning from keeping a trigger-locked shotgun stashed in the closet to carrying a loaded handgun downtown is a big step. And should I really be allowed to carry a firearm at the farmers' market after forgetting to unlock my weapon while accosting burglars? On the other hand, no matter how long the odds, I stubbornly resist the idea of being forced to rely on hope and timing as the only means of self-defense for my family—including in a public setting.

Perhaps the most responsible thing for me to do would be to take more training from Dan Marcon. You wouldn't know it from the bellicose posts on his Facebook page, but in his classes, Marcon stresses the "Nike defense"—no matter what kind of weapon you're packing, whenever safely possible, run away from trouble. Amen to that; unless cornered by circumstance, I much prefer to live like a peaceable fraidy cat.

When it comes to firearms, there's a lot of big-belly bluster going around. This leads me to think of my father, and about how he showed me the perforated pop cans, quietly leading me to understand the deadly responsibility at hand.

I don't know yet if I'm going to carry. But I'm sure not going to advertise the fact on my T-shirt.

In fact, I'd prefer that you wonder.

My one revolver is a Ruger Super Redhawk .44 Magnum with a seven-inch barrel. Bought it during a stretch of trouble with some bears. I can carry it, but I'll be danged if I can conceal it.

Recently my brother John's wife bought him a .357 that he carries holstered at his waist. It's a tidy little hammerless revolver with a laser sight. I decided to price one out.

On a sunny spring afternoon, I went to a local gun shop, a place where you can also get your transmission fixed. The owner, Larry, and I went to high school together. I told him I was writing a piece about guns. With a pistol on his hip he smiled and said quietly, "Well, as long as you get your facts straight."

Larry didn't have the .357 in stock, but I noticed a youth-size .410 shotgun in the rack. No matte black pistol grips, no pink inlays, just a serviceable little firearm. This year my 12-year-old daughter asked me to enroll her in a hunter's safety course. The .410 is a good starter gun with very little kick. And the youth model is much shorter. Not the greatest stopping power, but easier to handle in a confined space.

Say, for instance, the upstairs hallway.

Larry rang it up, and I headed home to the family.

2013

P.S. Within a short time of this piece being published, a man kicked down the door of my brother's small northern Wisconsin home. It was after midnight and my brother and his wife were asleep just feet away. Later, my brother said, "I figured I had two choices: dial 911 or .357." He went with the second choice first, and held the intruder for 55 minutes, which is how long it took for the deputies to arrive.

ALIVE, DEAD,
AND IN BETWEEN

HEALTH SECRETS FROM THE MORGUE

*When this piece was published it was accompanied by pho-
tos and the following caution: Warning! Graphic content.
View at your own discretion.*
   They weren't lying. You might wanna skip it.

I've been invited to watch someone pull the guts from a dead
man. The man has died, as they say, before his time. He was in
his 40s. If you want to know why young men die young—and
you'd like to avoid the same fate yourself—it makes sense to look
over the shoulder of someone like Michael Stier, MD. Dr. Stier is
a forensic pathologist often called as an expert witness in court
cases, and I am meeting him in a morgue near the University of
Wisconsin medical school, where he is an assistant professor. In
a short while, Dr. Stier will be up to his wrists in a fleshy cavity
containing organs that only a few hours ago pulsed and squeezed
and lent animation to a man's body.

   It's been some 15 years since I last observed an autopsy. I was
in training as an emergency medical responder, and the morgue
was located in a hospital in Eau Claire, Wisconsin. The man on
the table was young. He had gone on a bender and died of exposure after wandering into the woods on a cold night. I carry only
a few images: his shriveled gonads like misshapen gray clay, the
medical examiner slicing the liver like a loaf of bread, and—in the
only part of the procedure that struck me as creepy—the man's
scalp being peeled up and rolled over his face.

Since then, I have observed and handled dead bodies of all sorts—from shooting victims to mangled loggers—so I'm not overly concerned about puking on Dr. Stier's plastic clogs. Still, it's one thing to observe mutilation while amped on adrenaline; it is quite another to watch as a body is methodically turned inside out and the organs removed, sorted, and filleted. You have to steel yourself a bit.

Generally, preventing your own untimely demise is simple enough (buckle up and slow down, for starters), but pathologists pick up on dead-man trends the rest of us never contemplate. They know you may not be doing all you can to avoid the horizontal refrigerator. They know that even if you are ripped or can run five miles, you may still be at risk of a fatal heart attack. They know that one of the most cunning killers of men hides out in the brain and can't be seen with a microscope. I'm interested in the outcome of Dr. Stier's autopsy, but above all I hope to gather clues as to how I might postpone my own. Some of these clues will be in the corpse, but, as in any good detective story, the best of the rest I plan to gather from men who work the beat.

Andrew Baker, MD, chief medical examiner for Hennepin County, Minnesota, an area that includes Minneapolis, gives me my first lead: When he pulls back the sheet, the face staring back at him is usually that of a man.

"We see men of all ages with much greater frequency than we see women," he says. "That's taking all comers: gunshot wounds, drug overdoses, suicides, car crashes, and the occasional truly natural death of someone under 40."

What do we, as men in the full bloom of life, have most to fear?

Ourselves, apparently.

Dr. Stier's case—a man discovered dead in his garage—is still a lump waiting inside a black body bag when I emerge from the locker room in my scrubs. An assistant hands me a face shield and offers an odor-filtering mask. I detect a warm, sort of brown smell, right on the edge of foul. I once worked with a paramedic who entered a house around Thanksgiving and got hungry at the aroma of turkey—then went off it for years when he discovered an old man dead for days, with his forearm slow-roasting on a portable heater. I take the mask.

Dr. Stier arrives 10 minutes later, fresh from a morning workout. "I've been working on my abs real hard," he says. Of medium height and stocky build, he explains that he recently dropped 35 pounds. Swimming, mostly. "See these?" he says, pulling a pair of XXL scrub pants from a pile. "They used to special-order them for me." Dr. Stier, 38, tends to lock his hazel eyes on you when he speaks. It is the gaze of a man used to looking at bad things without flinching.

Before examining the body, Dr. Stier stops to speak with a police detective who has photographs of the death scene. The dead man had been working on his pickup truck and appeared to have been asphyxiated by carbon monoxide. But the photographs reveal raw red patches on the man's torso. Uncertain about the source of these injuries, the detective has come along to view the autopsy. "We're wondering if he might have been struck or burned," he says. When Dr. Stier's assistant unzips the body bag, the face that emerges is grossly swollen, and the tongue is protruding. Now and then a bloody bubble of escaping gas squeezes from the lips.

Dr. Stier circles the body while speaking into a handheld recorder, describing what he sees. When I ask him what he's looking for, he says, "Everything." It's important not to zero in on the obvious and overlook something critical—hand injuries not consistent with mechanical work, for instance, or inconspicuous needle holes. He turns off the recorder long enough to tell the detective that the red marks are typical of the way skin loosens and "slips" during normal decomposition. He also points out that the dead man's skin is bright pink, a condition that can occur when hemoglobin—which normally carries oxygen in the blood—bonds instead with carbon monoxide. If the man had suddenly dropped dead—say, of cardiac arrest—he wouldn't have breathed in all that carbon monoxide.

The vehicle's gas tank was empty, and there were tools scattered about, but it's hard to imagine even a weekend mechanic working on a running car in a closed garage for more than a few minutes. There are other possibilities. Perhaps he had a stroke and was unable to move. "Or," says Dr. Stier, pointing to the photo of the scattered tools, "people sometimes disguise their own suicide scene to make it look like an accident."

It's those sudden "natural deaths" Dr. Baker mentioned that make a guy want to reach for his wrist and check his pulse. According to Randy Hanzlick, MD, a professor at Emory University and the chief medical examiner of Fulton County, Georgia, the majority are tied to a man's ticker. "Usually there's some sort of unsuspected or premature cardiovascular disease," he says. "Or there's drug use—cocaine, for instance—that has affected the heart over the long term. And, in a small number of cases, we don't find anything." The heart simply fails.

Dr. Baker's own hands-on examinations of cadaverous cardiac tissue have brought him to a similar conclusion. "The most common thing we see is just advanced coronary-artery disease that men didn't know they had," he says. "They're 35 years old, and their arteries look like they're 60."

What can cause a man's heart to grow so old so early? Most often, a demon in his DNA. "You really have to be concerned about a genetic component when you have heart disease that young," says Dr. Baker, adding that when he sees early-onset atherosclerosis, he'll apprise the family of the danger that may be lurking in their genes. That danger could be familial hyper-cholesterolemia (FH), a disorder that impairs the body's ability to remove cholesterol from the blood. It's estimated that 1 in 500 people has FH, though many cases go undiagnosed. Of the people in this group, significantly more young men than women will suffer what FH researchers describe as "premature cardiac death."

While an autopsy may be a lifesaver for the relatives of men felled by FH, it isn't exactly a frontline diagnostic tool. That's why it's recommended that all young men research their family's health history and have their cholesterol checked every five years, starting at age 20. Any man who rings up an LDL-cholesterol score of 200 milligrams per deciliter or higher—and isn't leading a sedentary, saturated-fat-filled existence—should ask his doctor for further tests, including genetic testing for mutations in the LDL receptor gene. Going home and getting naked is also in order. Men can uncover clues that they have FH by examining their elbows, knees, and buttocks for xanthomas, bumps that form when excess cholesterol piles up under the skin.

But if FH is difficult to diagnose, at least it's relatively straightforward to treat: A statin, that chemical antidote to high cholesterol, can help keep most afflicted men out of the morgue.

Dr. Stier's assistant picks up a scalpel and begins the autopsy by drawing an incision from the pubic bone to the sternum, where he bifurcates the incision, cutting toward each shoulder to form a Y. In the wake of the blade, skin and fat part with a delicate hiss and crackle. The assistant rolls the flesh back from the chest, then snips the ribs with a tool akin to pruning shears. The bones part with a wet crunch. When the last rib is cut, the assistant lifts the shield-shaped chest plate away to expose the thoracic space, then drapes open the belly skin to reveal the contents of the abdomen. Meanwhile, Dr. Stier is sucking fluid from one of the cadaver's eyeballs with a large-gauge needle. Because the eyes absorb drugs and alcohol at a different rate than blood does, the fluid can sometimes help determine the time of death.

The exposed innards are mostly all reds and yellows. It is bracing to be reminded of all the organs we carry packed within us, churning away no matter whether we are sleeping, eating, or driving screws into decking. The space management alone is fascinating—the way the heart nestles between the lungs, the way the lower lobes of the lungs curve above the diaphragm, the way the diaphragm curves above the liver. Dr. Stier draws the final blood sample and then straightens. "Now," he says, "we take everything out."

The organ-sorting portion of the autopsy is workmanlike, and fairly speedy. One by one, each is cut loose, removed, and weighed, with the results posted on a chalkboard at the foot of the table: SPLEEN 100 g, R KIDNEY 200 g, L KIDNEY 250 g, HEART 300 g, and so on. Before placing an organ on a steel tray for dissection, Dr. Stier examines it visually. "Sometimes you open a suicide victim and find advanced cancer," he says. "People get the diagnosis and end their lives because they can't face the treatment or don't want to deal with the course of the disease."

Some of the organs—the lungs and liver, for instance—hold their shape well, while others, like the stomach (which Dr. Stier empties and checks for pills; there are none), look like so much uncooked meat. Because he was a lifelong smoker, the man's lymph nodes are stained brown, and his lungs are stippled with anthracotic pigment—clotty black rivulets that lend the lungs the speckled look of a rainbow trout. Three feet down the table, Dr. Stier's assistant is "running" the small intestine: stripping it out of the abdomen, checking every inch for abnormalities, and then spooling it into a plastic bucket.

Dr. Stier holds the dead man's heart in one hand; in the other he holds a small knife, with which he slices crosswise through the left anterior descending artery every two or three millimeters, creating a series of small serrations. "When a man dies prematurely of a heart attack, this is the artery most likely to be obstructed," he says. "We call it the 'widowmaker.'" It looks nothing like the red rubber tube so fulsomely rendered in American Heart Association brochures. After each cut, Dr. Stier rolls the blade over as if he were laying out a slice of cheese. Section after section, the artery is clear of the pasty white-yellow gloop you'd expect from a man who died while carrying a pack of cigarettes. "A drinker without cirrhosis is more common than a smoker without atherosclerosis," says Dr. Stier, plainly delighted to point out an exception to the rule.

Sometimes the crushing pain in a man's chest isn't a heart attack but a pulmonary embolism, in which a blood clot travels from one part of the body (usually the lower leg) to block an artery in the lung. But while the source of the symptom may be different, many times the end result is the same: an early exit.

"The youngest I've seen was 17," says Dr. Stier. "Usually there were risk factors, including extended periods of immobility—such as an airplane flight—or an injury like a severe sprain or fracture that required immobilization in a splint or cast."

Even though the flying-is-dying connection to pulmonary embolisms is the most well known—their frequency prompted doctors to coin the term "economy-class syndrome"—some researchers believe that a desk job can be just as dangerous. Last year, scientists in New Zealand reported on four cases in which young men developed either a pulmonary embolism or deep-vein thrombosis—the initial formation of a clot—after remaining seated at a computer for between three and six hours at a clip. The researchers even came up with their own catchy name for the phenomenon: "seated immobility thromboembolism," their contortion to arrive at the acronym SIT.

The only good news about this white-collar man killer is how simple it is to prevent. If you tend to get glued to your CPU, take regular walking breaks. If you spend your life at 35,000 feet, drink water (dehydration increases the risk) and walk the aisle every two hours. And if you're seatbelt bound? Press your heels against the cabin floor several times an hour to help push blood through your calves. As a bonus, a recent study in the *International Journal of Cardiology* shows that such isometric exercises can reduce high blood pressure—another invisible menace that attacks men much earlier than it strikes women and can put us on the fast track to a formaldehyde injection.

Dr. Stier asks me to move in closer as he prepares to cut up the dead man's liver, which is mottled with yellowish tan patches. "The liver should be reddish brown," he says, while running his gloved finger over the surface. "See how it's greasy? Almost oily? These are signs of alcohol damage. If you stop drinking at this stage, the liver will heal, but once scar tissue accumulates, the changes are permanent." Dr. Stier's knife moves through the organ smoothly—in more advanced liver disease, it can be physically difficult to push the blade. Long-term alcohol abuse can also ruin the pancreas, causing it to shrink and harden until it has a chalky feel. Dr. Stier checks, and the man's pancreas appears normal.

With most of the chest and abdominal cavity empty, the deflated tube of the descending aorta is visible. Dr. Stier slits it lengthwise. The aorta falls open to reveal smooth, curdlike protuberances clinging to the wall like clumps of egg white. These are atherosclerotic plaques, and seeing them up close, I wonder how many I'm growing. These are in no danger of blocking the aorta—it's roughly the diameter of a garden hose—but you can see how they would be deadly in a cardiac artery.

I notice that Dr. Stier's assistant has placed one hand on the crown of the dead man's cranium. In the other hand he holds a scalpel, and as he runs it ear-to-ear across the back of the man's head, I prepare for the sound of the bone saw.

If you spend enough time stuffing people into the back end of an ambulance, as I have, it's bound to alter your behavior. I love motorcycles, but you'll never catch me astride one—at the last crack-up I responded to, I had to pull slivers of femur out of a car door.

Having seen people killed as they were getting the mail, I also wear my bicycle helmet for the one-block ride to the post office. If I take the car three blocks to the gas station, I wear a seatbelt. My experience with the local fire department has left me with a pathological aversion to electric space heaters. On issues of personal safety, I am, frankly, a fussbudget. And yet, on the personal-health front—Exhibit A: late-night gas-station doughnut binges—I constantly lapse into bad habits. Perhaps if I spent five days a week taking dead people apart to see why they died, I would take better care of my own insides.

"I try to eat as healthy as I can," says Dr. Baker. "I run, bike, and swim, and obviously I would never take up cigarette smoking or drink excessively. The average person would think smoking is a bad idea, but for a forensic pathologist, that point is reinforced day after day." The doctor also makes a point of seeing a doctor. "I see my own internist," says Dr. Baker. "I want someone who takes care of living people counseling me about my weight, my exercise, and my cholesterol."

Dr. Hanzlick's perspective is even more intriguing. He admits his job has little impact on his diet and personal behavior, but it has made him less comfortable about heights. "I think it has to do with seeing people over the years who have fallen off high structures. Oh, and lightning bothers me now, too." His fears are not unfounded: According to the National Oceanic and Atmospheric Administration and the Centers for Disease Control and Prevention, 84 percent of lightning fatalities are male—most between 20 and 44 years of age.

It's relatively easy to get at the organs in your abdomen and thorax. Your brain, on the other hand, is in a lockbox. Dr. Stier's assistant buzzes around the circumference of the cranium with a bone saw and tips the skullcap back as if it's on a hinge. Dr. Stier puts a hand on each side of the cerebrum and lifts it like custard from a Jell-O mold. The brain is beginning to decompose and comes apart in Dr. Stier's hands as he searches for any evidence of infection, cancer, trauma, or bleeding. He finds nothing abnormal. The brain is weighed and dissected, and the skullcap and scalp are replaced.

Of all the organs that can kill a young man, the brain ranks high. For one thing, it is responsible for decisions like "Hey! Let's bumper-surf naked!" But Dr. Baker warns that the male brain often incubates another deadly danger. "Untreated depression is a significant part of many of the deaths we see. Just as I would not want young men to blow off chest pain, I'd hate for them not to get their depression treated, whether because of finances or social stigma."

The stats bear him out: Men are four times more likely to die as a result of suicide than women are. Some guys, of course, are more at risk than others. In a 2005 study from Johns Hopkins, researchers discovered that even though male physicians tend to adopt healthy behaviors that give them mortality rates 56 percent lower than the rest of us, they're much more likely to write out their own death certificates.

"I think it's stress related," says Dr. Stier. "Doctors are overachievers surrounded by overachievers. I see it in my med students—if they have problems, they try to mask them. That mindset continues into practice." Mix in the male propensity for suicide and an educated understanding of the most effective methods of death, and you have the recipe for some serious malpractice.

If this were *CSI: Wisconsin,* Dr. Stier would have his a-HA! moment about now. As it is, we are left to speculate. All signs point to carbon monoxide poisoning (the toxicology results are necessary to make a definitive call), but was this man a victim of bad luck or careful planning? "I determine cause of death," says Dr. Stier, a pathologist. "The coroner establishes the manner of death." Armed with Dr. Stier's report, the coroner will interview the deceased's family and friends in a search for clues. Intentionally or accidentally, the man is dead. The assistant tucks the organs inside the human rind, stitches up the Y, and rolls the body from the room.

When I walk out of the morgue and into the light of a bright fall morning, it's good to see the sun. The signs of wear I saw in that man—the mottled liver, the clumps in his aorta—hadn't killed him, but they were hard evidence of what we accumulate over time and through denial. Above all, that paradoxically healthy cardiac artery niggled at me. Do my arteries look like that? Or are they crammed with sludge? I have never smoked, but my last two cholesterol tests were high and higher.

First thing tomorrow morning, I'll report to my general practitioner for a thorough physical. Once you've seen someone's guts in a bucket, it's difficult to think of your skin as anything but a bag full of trouble.

2006

P.S. I got that physical. Now I'm a couple years overdue again. Human nature is a killer.

HUMAN POPSICLES

I always back into parking spots. It facilitates the quick getaway. I have cultivated this habit based on the example of the local fire chief, my own low-level paranoia, and the practice of a Vietnam vet of my acquaintance who never leaves home without his sidearm and a percolating case of post-traumatic stress disorder.

When I chose my spot in the parking lot outside 7895 East Acoma Drive in Scottsdale, Arizona, on a sunny afternoon last fall, backing in was a no-brainer. I was in investigative-journalist mode, and word on the street (plus any number of major media outlets) had it that the frozen body of baseball great Ted Williams was being stored at this address, in a building owned by the Alcor Life Extension Foundation. Alcor "freezes" people. Whole, and in part. It currently plays host to 12 frozen humans, 37 frozen human heads, and a few miscellaneous frozen pets. If Ted Williams is in there, he is not alone.

Alcor has been in the human Popsicle business—they prefer the term "cryonic suspension"—for 30 years. A full-body suspension costs $120,000. If that's a little too rich for your blood (which, by the by, will be drained and replaced with antifreeze), you can try to get your life insurance to pick up the tab, or you can opt for a neurosuspension, in which Alcor will detach and freeze your head for $50,000. The idea, in a nutshell, is to freeze you and keep you frozen until science figures out a way to undo what did you in.

The concept of preserving people to keep till later is not a new one. It pops up regularly in books and film, but most main-stream media references have been framed in a "News of the Weird" context. While Walt Disney is frequently cited as the most famous person ever frozen, the best evidence suggests that he was cremated upon his death in 1966. The Disney myth may have been spawned by the coincidence of his dying within a few weeks of a press conference announcing the formation of the Cryonics Society of California.

Generally recognized as the first official cryonics organization, the Cryonics Society of California set the standard against which all other cryonics organizations would be measured. Turns out that standard was below ground level and rather damp. Founder Robert Nelson stored his clients in a subterranean crypt in Chatsworth, California, eventually ran out of money, and, in what became known as "The Chatsworth Incident," allegedly let dozens of bodies thaw. Police investigations and lawsuits followed. Cultivating mainstream acceptance is an uphill battle when your movement is associated with a capitalized Incident and the phrase "subterranean crypt."

Alcor has been trying to prevent its own public-relations melt-down ever since Ted Williams died last July. Ted's son claimed the slugger wished to be frozen. Ted's daughter said he wanted to be cremated. Alcor won't say yea or nay, but it is generally accepted that A Certain Baseball Legend is cooling his heels in the back room, waiting for extra innings.

It was a story loaded with blockbuster ingredients: dead sports hero, bitter family feud, intimations of immortality. To say nothing of the fact that there is just something about storing humans by the freezerful that freaks out the unfrozen majority. What kind of people want to be frozen? Even more than that, what kind of people agree to ice these people down? And why do it in Scottsdale, where summer temperatures can reach 120 degrees?

Many questions, some of them creepy. And so I have driven to an industrial park on the north edge of the city and am lurking outside Alcor headquarters. Lurking is a little futile when the

car-rental company sticks you in a bright red four-door Oldsmo-
bile Alero. I did do a little drive-by before parking, just to check
the look of the place. A modest gray building with ALCOR across
the facade. Next door, a sewing shop. In the parking lot, your
typical assortment of cars cooking in the Arizona sun. Nothing
unusual. Unless you count the bumper sticker on the minivan two
spots over: *This vehicle will be frozen until the mechanic figures
out how to fix it.*

I am met at the door by Bill Haworth, Alcor's public-relations con-
sultant. A middle-aged former Marine with close-cropped brown
hair, Haworth is a specialist in crisis communications, exactly
what Alcor needed for the Ted Williams situation. "A member of
a baseball legend's family said we were selling DNA from our patients," he tells me. "There was no logic to it—it would be much
more difficult to obtain DNA from someone in suspension than
to take a skin sample when he was still alive." In other words,
procuring the genetic code from a suspended Ted would require
an ice pick.

Haworth shows me into the skylighted main room. In the center is a glass table holding 19 framed portraits and one Emmy
Award. The portraits include uniformed soldiers, a married couple, a man identified only as FM-2030 ("FM" stands for "Future
Man"), a long-haired young man playing electric bass, and Dick
Clair. Clair was a writer on *The Carol Burnett Show*. The Emmy is
his. Until Ted Williams came along, Clair was Alcor's number-one
celebrity endorsement.

Next, Haworth introduces me to Jerry Lemler, MD, president,
CEO, and medical director of Alcor. He's a balding fellow of medium height, with a trim beard and wire-rimmed glasses. A former
practicing psychiatrist, the 52-year-old Dr. Lemler received the
Exemplary Psychiatrist Award from the National Alliance for the
Mentally Ill in 1994, the same year he began to think about immortality. It was a Saturday, and Dr. Lemler was sitting on a rug in

the mud at Woodstock '94, listening to Joe Cocker. As Cocker left the stage, he hollered, "See you at Woodstock III . . . in 2019!" Dr. Lemler says the moment was "premonitory" and left him blindsided by the idea of his own mortality.

"Joe Cocker lit a fire in me," says Dr. Lemler.

The doctor began to entertain the idea of death as optional. When he read Dr. Eric Drexler's *Engines of Creation*—cited by many cryonophiles as the impetus for their conversion—he came to believe cryonics was the key to outwitting mortality. "People who won't have to die from disease are crawling—not walking—the planet today," he says. "Most of us won't live to see that. The only mechanism by which we might is cryonics."

You can't just drop Grandma in the freezer chest beside the bratwurst and hope to revive her for Thanksgiving 3000. Even if you vacuum-seal her in a jumbo FoodSaver bag, she will, like blueberries, be a little on the mushy side when thawed. That's because ice crystals expand as they form, ripping apart delicate cell structures. But by replacing a client's blood with a sort of antifreeze and then rapidly cooling the body to negative 120 degrees Fahrenheit, Alcor says it can minimize this damage. It's critical, though, to begin suspension procedures as quickly as possible, since decay begins the second you die. If too much time passes, the odds you'll wake up *Sleeper*-style next to an Orgasmatron dwindle to near zero.

As a client's checkout time approaches, the Alcor CryoTransport Team will fly or drive to the client's location to prepare for what Dr. Lemler very pointedly calls "our lifesaving procedures." After the client dies, the team hooks up an IV, then performs chest compressions to circulate a cocktail of medications designed to prevent clotting and minimize cell damage. After that, the body is packed in ice and shipped back to Scottsdale. What if a client dies unexpectedly? Sometimes Alcor officials find themselves on the phone, trying to convince a skeptical doctor to administer anticlotting medication to a dead person.

Dr. Lemler is twisting at a doorknob. He summons Bill Haworth. "Bill, could you find out who has the key to the operating room?" Haworth hustles away, his boot heels striking the tiles with a corky echo.

The operating room is small but not cramped. "This is where the patient is placed," says Dr. Lemler, motioning toward a covered trough lined with a cooling pad. Once the patient is in the trough, his blood is pumped out and replaced with cryoprotectant. To monitor the process—called perfusion—an Alcor technician drills a hole in the patient's skull. One techie told me a healthy brain will reduce in diameter by as much as three-quarters of an inch. I ask him what sort of device was used to measure brain size. "We eyeball it," he says.

I spot a Plexiglas box the size of a large hibachi, with four heavy-duty threaded pins, pointy ends inward. "Is that where they cool the heads?" I ask. "Yes," says Dr. Lemler. "It's called cephalic isolation." I conjure up a cranium chilling to minus 120 degrees. I get a twinge, a kind of sympathetic ice-cream headache.

Back to the trough. Through the gradual circulation of liquid nitrogen, the patient's temperature is lowered to 390 degrees below zero. Then the body is wrapped, placed into a pod, and, with the help of a crane, lowered headfirst into a tank. The toes-up position is predicated on Alcor's belief that the brain is the source of human identity. If a tank springs a leak, the body will thaw from toe to head, sparing the brain until the last. All Alcor clients sign a contract stating that in the event of an accidental thaw, Alcor may detach their heads and toss the remaining remains.

So what kind of person wants to be cryonically preserved? Bill Haworth gives me the name of Blaine Repsher, a 20-year-old who's attending community college in Tucson. I feel a little funny calling him, like I'm gawking over my cell phone.

Repsher says people find out when they see his silver medical bracelet. "Everyone always asks, 'Oh, do you have diabetes or something?' And I'm like, 'Well, no, I'm going to be frozen when I die.'"

The bracelet (standard issue to Alcor members) is embossed with a caduceus and a little red cross, and engraved with instructions that essentially tell emergency medical personnel to call Alcor—collect if necessary—should the patient croak.

"Some people think it's a waste of time," Repsher says when I ask how folks react to his deep-freeze plan. "Others think it's pretty cool." He pauses, then adds, "I had a girlfriend who didn't like it too much. She told me it was ridiculous and wasn't going to happen."

Repsher was in seventh grade when he registered with Alcor. "My parents were signed up when I was 10," he says. "I never really considered death, then my grandma passed away, and it got me thinking more along those lines. I asked my parents if there was any way I could sign up."

I ask Repsher if he ponders life in the future. "I do sometimes," he replies. "I'd like to see what kind of technology would exist. You'd always hope for flying cars and stuff like that, but I don't know . . . "

Repsher is a Buck Rogers optimist. Me, I'm more of a Mad Max pessimist. I have this sneaking suspicion that upon emerging from my tank I'd want to crawl right back in.

"Bill?" Dr. Lemler needs another key. We are standing at the very back of the Alcor building, before a large sliding door with a smaller door inset. This is it. I'm about to get a look at Alleged Ted Central.

It's an unremarkable room. Cement floor. Cement-block walls. The tanks are arranged around the perimeter. Dewars, they're called. Pronounced do-er. As in, Who-er in the do-er? Ted's in there, I think. Ted. In a tank.

The dewars come in two sizes. The larger ones—the staff calls them "Bigfoots"—are nine feet tall and roughly the circumference of a large water heater. Each sports a large blue-and-white decal featuring the Alcor logo, slogan ("Since 1972"), and Web address. The smaller dewars—there are two—are used for storing heads only, and are roughly the size of Luciano Pavarotti.

"You can fit up to four whole bodies and five heads—nine total patients—into a Bigfoot," says Dr. Lemler. "The smaller dewars hold eight heads each." He waves at the tanks. "The heads outnumber the whole bodies by about three to one, in part because neural suspension is less expensive, and in part because we believe that any technology capable of resuscitation will be capable of generating a new body."

I scan the room. "It's pretty nondescript," says Dr. Lemler, "but the room is double-fortified with concrete, and for every lock and alarm you see, there are motion detectors and light sensors you'll never see. From time to time we do employ security, especially when there may be someone of note here." I wait for him to give a meaningful nod toward one of the dewars. It doesn't happen.

When I asked Dr. Lemler about the idea of freezing people in Arizona, he told me the temperature was moot. "Arizona is a climatically and geologically safe area. Tornadoes are very, very rare. No earthquakes to speak of. We're on firm footing here," he says.

But are they? Even if Alcor avoids a dewar-cracking natural disaster, can cryonic suspension really work? Aby J. Mathew, PhD, director of hypothermic preservation services for BioLife Solutions, says the biggest obstacle to overcome is, well, bigness. "Right now you can cryopreserve individual cells relatively well. But when you get to an organ or an entire being, you have so many different layers of cells, you can't get those inner levels freezing at the same rate as the outer levels."

"It would not be correct for us to say it's crazy," adds Mathew. "And we would not necessarily discount the possibility that if we preserve people now, future technologies may be able to resuscitate and regenerate them."

Many cryonics supporters, including Dr. Lemler, believe that the regeneration problem will be solved by nanotechnology. Using molecule-size medical tools, doctors will be able to repair a body one cell at a time. Experts such as Kristen Kulinowski, PhD, executive director of the Center for Biological and Environmental Nanotechnology at Rice University, are not so sure.

"This is like asking whether a toddler can run a marathon. The child can barely walk. The point is that nanotechnology is in its infancy, like a toddler," says Kulinowski. "I'm not going to say it's impossible, but I wouldn't want to make any bets."

Michael Shermer, PhD, the publisher of *Skeptic* magazine, is less generous. In a piece he wrote for *Scientific American,* he equated "your brain on cryonics" to mushy, thawed strawberries. "Even if they find a way to repair the cellular damage, no one has any clue how to restart the motor, other than a Frankensteinian thing where you just electrocute it and see what happens," he says.

"Most of the practitioners are realistic about its probability of working," he adds. "It's not like these are cranks scamming people out of a lot of money. They're not."

He thinks for a moment. "I guess if they'd give me a free freeze, I'd go for it. I hear they offered one to Isaac Asimov and he turned it down. I wouldn't turn down a free freeze."

When the tour's over, I head for the rental car. It's warm inside. Being from northern Wisconsin, I like things warm. I wait a bit before hitting the air conditioner. When I finally switch it on, it feels a little harsh.

I imagine myself hanging in the tank, as cold as the planet Pluto. I have the ice-cream pain again. But I'm over the idea of cryonics as some sort of creepy secret. Dunking someone in liquid nitrogen isn't really any stranger than the other socially acceptable things we do with the dead. Seems to me Alcor's clients are simply operating on the theory that they have nothing to lose. They're buying a $120,000 lottery ticket.

I check in with Bill Haworth a month later. He seems a little strained. Says we need to wrap things up, because Alcor is going into a "total media blackout." Sounds intriguing.

I wonder if maybe there is a new legal development in the whole Ted thing. Or maybe, just maybe, they're onto something big.

Ladies and gentlemen, now batting . . .

2003

P.S. Publication of this piece was somewhat complicated by the fact that one of the longtime employees of Alcor has the same name as I.

PUKING

Apart from orgasm, no other natural human function overtakes our mental and physical faculties as thoroughly as a woofing good puke. I recently barfed with such vigor that both my nasal passages became impenetrably jammed with chicken nuggets.

In part because I've always been teetotal, my personal puking experience is unremarkable, limited mostly to run-of-the mill gargle sessions courtesy of the flu. I did once puke courtesy of a lukewarm inflight enchilada provided to me by a major airline. Then again, one suspects the willful ingestion of an enchilada halfheartedly rewarmed at 35,000 feet is by definition a form of self-induced vomiting.

When not puking myself, I have studied the puking of others. For 15 years now, I have worked as an EMT, and while I'd love to project a more heroic image, I must say that in the field of medical rescue, puke is the great constant. Sick people puke, dying people puke, excited people puke, people puke while they're having heart attacks, they puke when their lacerated brains swell, they puke because they get carsick lying on the ambulance cot looking up at the dome lights. Shoot, I have seen entire families puke purely out of solidarity. Ma blows potatoes across the bathroom, and Dad and the kids lean over and hurl in unison. The sympathy puke, we call it.

And that's the complicated beauty of puking. It's so much more than a symptom of illness. Puking is a form of self-expression. It comes from the gut, yes, but it also comes from the soul. And sometimes, the heels.

Pursuant to my vomit contemplations, I resolved to consult experts on the subject, but because I so rarely attend birthing classes, fraternity hazings, or breakfast with hungover waif supermodels, I settled for a Web search. Vomit is a subject tailor-made for the Web. In short order I had turned up a slew of revolting jpegs, a handful of jaw-dropping mpegs, and reams of barfisms. Still, it was all so superficial, so thumbnail. I needed depth. Science. I turned to the folks who wrote the book on vomiting. Or, more specifically, the "technical review" on vomiting, as approved by the American Gastroenterological Association (AGA) and published in the January 2001 issue of *Gastroenterology.*

The AGA defines vomiting as "forceful oral expulsion of gastric contents associated with contraction of the abdominal and chest wall musculature." Feeling, perhaps, that this description lacked punch, the authors revisit the subject three sentences later and punch up the prose, this time defining the central act as "a highly specific physical event that results in the rapid, forceful evacuation of gastric contents in retrograde fashion from the stomach up to and out of the mouth." Or, to put it another way, gastroenterologists can spank a thesaurus with the best of them. Although why they settled for "mouth" when "buccal cavity" was the obvious choice, I do not know.

Merck Manual, the bible of hypochondriacs everywhere, breaks vomiting down into two types: physiologic and psychogenic. Physiologic vomiting occurs as the result of identifiable forces acting on the body, from tumors of the inner ear to bad shrimp to bad shrimp boat rides. When you eat that piece of hinky shrimp, it produces toxins that enter the bloodstream and travel to the brain, where they trigger any of the five or so chemoreceptors capable of precipitating vomiting. Psychogenic vomiting, on the other hand, is precipitated by abstract elements such as fear, repulsion, or even profound anger. Which is why your average IRS auditor is a little twitchy. The *Merck Manual* even goes so far as to indicate that psychogenic vomiting can be a sign of hostility. Not pent-up hostility, obviously. And again, bad news for the IRS.

Most of the time, vomiting is a good and necessary thing. On the other hand, it may represent something more dire. The AGA lists more than 100 vomit triggers, including cancer, bowel obstruction, nicotine, strokes, Jamaican vomiting sickness, ear infections, closed head injuries, heart attacks and, paradoxically, starvation. Vomiting, as it turns out, is the symptom for all seasons. Persistent vomiting, or vomiting in the absence of nausea, or vomit containing blood or dark "coffee grounds" type material (older blood), is worthy of a doctor's attention. In general, however, your main concern with vomiting is how to keep hydrated and avoid chipping your teeth on the toilet bowl.

Vomiting-related injuries are rare, but puke hard enough and you can blow a gasket. Or an esophageal artery, a nasty development doctors call Mallory-Weiss syndrome. The primary risk factors for incurring Boerhaave syndrome, a potentially deadly puke-induced rupture of the esophagus, are alcoholism and overindulgence in food and drink, which begs the question, why not rename it the much-easier-to-pronounce NFL Stadium Parking Lot Pregame Tailgate Party Syndrome? And then there is the more recently recognized condition called prolapsed gastropothy. Mid-barf, the upper end of the stomach collapses and is sucked up into the lower part of the esophagus. When you're not around, board-certified gastroenterologists refer to this condition as Puking Your Guts Out.

We do give it our all. We've all had that moment when we realized—right mid-hurl—that if we did crunches of this intensity on a regular basis, we would develop abs like marble speed bumps. By way of contrast, consider dogs, masters of the dispassionate puke. With a minimum of sound effects and hunching, they bring up supper, and just as quickly, put it back down. As if relief of the upset stomach is simply an issue of rearranging the gastric feng shui. Even cats hacking up hairballs don't slump to the floor when it's over.

Some animals—including mice and rats—don't puke at all. The oldest recorded vomit—160 million years old—was discovered last year in an English clay pit, right where a dyspeptic ichthyosaur left it. I wonder if he gripped the sides of the pit with his flippers, got right down there, his scaly head hanging, his snoot dripping. *Praying Wisconsin-style,* as a friend once put it.

"Nausea and vomiting give us an evolutionary advantage," says Dr. David Fleisher, MD, director of the Division of Pediatric Gastroenterology at the University of Missouri School of Medicine. "If we eat green meat, we vomit. The next time we see green meat, we don't eat it. This keeps us from repeating the same mistakes. It is very common in pediatrics, for example, where if a kid goes to McDonald's and for some reason throws up there he will never go to another McDonald's again. Or he gets nauseated every time he passes that particular restaurant." Which would explain why you so rarely see George Bush Sr. at Benihana.

Evolutionary advantages aside, the human puking mode still seems unfair. If we must get "sick as a dog," why can't we "vomit like a dog"? How—in contrast to our own spasmodic chunk-blasting—do dogs manage to puke with such insouciance? "When I was in medical school, in my pharmacology course the professor got a dog and put him in front of the lecture hall and injected him with morphine, which is very emetogenic, and the dog shivered and puked and then it was over," says Dr. Fleisher. "If a dog sees something that is disgusting, it doesn't vomit. If I was a dog I would be disgusted all day long, but dogs don't get disgusted."

This helps in *eating* the puke, I suppose, which is the obvious drawback to doing things the dog way. In the name of research, the 18th-century Italian naturalist Lorenzo Spallanzani studied human digestion by eating his own vomit, bringing it up again, noting any changes in consistency, eating it again, bringing it up, and so on, ad nauseam.

• • •

I was driving past a junkyard the day those chicken nuggets got the better of me. Driven by a physiologic urge, I pulled over, ducked between a pair of crumpled four-doors, and began to dispense chicken bits in a retrograde fashion. "Ohhh, not out the nose," I remember thinking.

Kneeling weakly after the storm had passed, I tried to blow the nuggets clear. Nothing. Only one option: The dreaded retro-snork. I steeled myself, then snorked. The result was an immediate conversion from physiogenic to psychogenic vomiting triggered by disgust. I became locked in a horrific Spallanzanian loop: Snork, hurl, snork, hurl, snork, hurl. Minutes passed. The cycle was broken only upon the eventual depletion of nuggets. I knelt there, drooling and snot-ridden, eyes watering and bloodshot, rib and stomach muscles burning, teeth etched and bitter, nose stinging . . .

What I'm saying is, I was feeling a lot better.

2003

P.S. It's funny to read through these and find dated references. Does today's reader get the George Bush Sr. and Benihana reference (he once threw up on the Japanese prime minister) or know of the Merck Manual *now that WebMD is transcendent?*

Puking, on the other hand, is timeless.

MIKE IS SWEATY

I am naked as a skinless breast of chicken, breaded head to toe in golden cornstarch, and about to be slipped inside an oven the size of a small shed. Robert D. Fealey, MD, the Mayo Clinic neurologist and engineer who designed the oven, has just informed me that the cornstarch is cut with a chemical called alizarin red. "Approved by the USDA for stamping meat," he says, tickled by the joke. As he swivels back to his computer monitors, Dr. Fealey addresses the nurse standing beside my gurney: "Okay, you can roll him in."

One out of six Americans think they sweat too much. I'm not sure if I do or not. Dr. Fealey is going to help me decide.

First, he will bake me like a biscuit.

You are the proud operator of up to five million sweat glands. Except for the odor-causing kind found in your pits, most of these exist to keep your body from boiling over. Whether you're grunting through the reps of an upper-body workout or simply basking on the beach, your sweat glands respond to temperature spikes by drawing water from the blood in your capillaries and pumping it (along with some salt and potassium) onto your skin. As each molecule of perspiration pops out, it begins to evaporate, stealing energy—in the form of heat—from your skin and leaving you cooler in the process.

The average guy just hanging out will lose 1 to 1.5 liters of sweat per day. Play a little pickup basketball or hammer on your mountain bike, however, and you can pump out 3 liters in a single hour. My personal world record for on-the-spot sweat production was set on an airplane bound for Denver. We had just been told to shut off our cellphones when I realized I couldn't find mine. I did a quick pat-down, rummaged through my bag, dug around in the cushions. Nothing. I felt that first low-level gut tickle and forehead prickle—same one the caveman felt when he got a whiff of saber-tooth spoor.

I scuttled up the jetway for a fast, fruitless search of the gate area, then hurried back to face 175 pairs of angry eyeballs. The captain came out of the cabin and ordered a flight attendant to dial my cell number—four times—while another attendant pulled up cushions, opened bin doors, and delivered a chatty play-by-play. We finally found the phone wedged deep between the seats. By this point sweat was slicking down my neck and chest and dripping from my forehead to my lap. Today, I can comfort myself with the knowledge that human sweat contains a naturally occurring antimicrobial agent, and that I had done future residents of seat 3B a favor by sanitizing the upholstery.

Alas, the same squeegee thing happens if a grocery checkout clerk decides to deliver color commentary on the contents of my cart: "Oooh! Rutabagas! Ham hocks! And nose-hair clippers!" I feel suddenly naked and become instantly sweaty.

How weird is that?

"Actually, it's fairly common," says Autumn Braddock, PhD, codirector of the Anxiety Disorders Clinic at the Mayo Clinic. "You're having a fear response during a social situation. Our bodies have been fine-tuned over the years to become intensely activated when we sense fear, and that activity generates heat, which in turn generates sweat." She also says some scientists hypothesize that "fear sweat" is designed to make you slippery and hard to grab. Thus ends many a blind date.

◆ ◆ ◆

Before I am dusted like a cinnamon doughnut for the thermoregulatory sweat test (TST), I tell Dr. Fealey about my tendency to sweat in the grocery line. He sits me in a swivel chair beside a black box roughly the size of a cash register and attaches moisture sensors to my palms and left forearm.

Three parallel lines—one per sensor—begin to ease across a nearby computer screen, straight and flat. "We're going to see how you sweat in response to emotional stimuli," says Dr. Fealey. With his graying but thick brown hair, his beard, and his herringbone suit coat, he could be a college professor. "Let's do some simple math exercises." I feel an instant prickle at the nape of my neck and above my brow. In my world, there are no simple math exercises. "Can you count back from 100 by sevens?" asks Dr. Fealey. "Ninety-three!" I say, triumphantly. But then I have to start carrying ones. "Eighty . . . errr . . . six?" I do math in my head as well as I do knitting with my feet. "Seventy-ummm . . ."

Dr. Fealey and his nurse are staring at me expectantly. I flash back to the day everyone gathered in the gym to watch Dixie Fuss beat me in the sixth-grade spelling bee. I sneak a peek at the computer screen. The two flat lines that had been tracing my palm sweat are spiking upward. Dr. Fealey is grinning triumphantly. About the time I mumble, "Ahhh . . . 51?" he lets me off the hook.

"We try to choose stimuli that will increase palmar sweating," says Dr. Fealey. "We look for the patient's emotional button."

I chuckle at how well the math trick worked.

"You're not a rocket scientist," Dr. Fealey replies.

I've been saying that for years.

The only thing worse than nervous sweating is nervous sweating caused by nervous sweating.

"We don't really know the exact mechanisms involved," says Braddock, "but if the thought pops into your mind that *Oh crap, I'm going to start sweating, and if I sweat now, that will be embarrassing,* you're again sending yourself the message that there's something 'dangerous' present. The idea that sweating is negative triggers a cascade of fear responses."

I was once invited to meet a famous person who had done me a good turn. I got lost on my way there, and by the time I was ushered into the man's office and reached out to shake his hand, I wondered if he could hear the swamp noises emanating from my armpits. Embarrassed, I felt the sweat pump out even faster. He was a tiny guy, and I felt like an oozing tower of lard.

"At the end of the day, what I hear most from men is that they are embarrassed," says Lisa Pieretti, executive director of the International Hyperhidrosis Society (IHHS), a nonprofit organization for people affected by excessive sweating. "Every letter I get, there's that word: embarrassed."

Of course, the problem isn't the sweat itself or even how much pours out of our pores, but rather where and when perspiration happens.

With sweat, context is everything.

For example, I was raised in rural Wisconsin, where a man's stature is established in part by his ability to roll logs or sling hay bales. I remember how it felt as a youngster to stand among the rugged crew after the work was done, each of them drenched in sweat, me feeling just a little closer to being a full-grown man thanks to my soggy T-shirt. A sweaty man had proven his worth.

I still get that feeling sometimes—I'll straighten from my toil, lean against the shovel, run my wrist across my brow, and squint against the sweat and sun, and I'll imagine I'm starring in a slow-motion commercial (perhaps for beer, perhaps for a diesel pickup truck) and any second now, some babe in a convertible will cruise by, her eyes locking on the droplet trickling from my pecs, tracing it as it zigzags down my abs. And maybe a delicate little bead breaks out on her upper lip and she touches it with her tongue . . . and then my wife asks me if for Pete's sake I've turned the compost yet.

Sweaty-guy-gets-lucky fantasies are fueled by the idea that sweat conveys erotic possibilities. Let us now praise the University of Pennsylvania study in which women who were exposed to the pheromones found in male perspiration felt less tense and more relaxed. The researchers obtained these results after applying extracts of male underarm secretions directly to the women's lips. Good luck with that.

Now I am in a human toaster oven, looking up at two cameras—one shoots me above the waist, one below. Dr. Fealey will be snapping pictures until—hopefully—the chemical interaction of alizarin red and Perry sweat turns me violet all over. "We want to see if there are any abnormalities in the pattern," he says. Unevenness or gaps can be an indicator of problems ranging from dermatitis to Parkinson's disease.

It's taking me longer to ramp up the dampness than I thought it would. The air-conditioning in the clinic had me fairly well chilled by the time I was called in, and then I had to disrobe in a tile bathroom. I can feel the glow of the thermoregulatory cabinet's 3.2-kilowatt quartz heaters, but so far, no sweat. Ironically enough, the cabinet is being piped full of cool jazz. Perhaps some Shakira would move things along.

For most of us, overblown sweating is an occasional inconvenience, but for many others—up to 3 percent of the population—hyperhidrosis is a debilitating clinical condition. Defined as excessive sweating beyond what the body requires, hyperhidrosis seems the stuff of a cheap cartoon gag. But for those afflicted, it is a condition with severe side effects. Medical literature contains reports of a military sharpshooter unable to handle his weapon and a man who couldn't attend meetings without soaking through his papers. Some people have to budget extra money just to replace frequently ruined clothing.

The majority who seek treatment, however, are driven by the social toll. A recent Harris survey sponsored by the IHHS shows that 66 percent of people thought a visibly sweaty person was nervous; 49 percent thought the person was overweight or out of shape; and 25 percent thought he (or she) was unhealthy. On the upside, 42 percent thought the heavy sweater was hardworking. Furthermore, half said extreme sweating in public was less embarrassing than passing gas, burping, leaving your fly open, or going bald.

Counting last month, I'm five for five.

Fortunately, we have treatment options for excessive sweating—more, in fact, than we have for baldness. Some men find relief with prescription antiperspirants like Drysol, but prolonged use can cause skin irritation. Some medications help, but they have to be taken two or three times a day and can leave you with cottonmouth, blurred vision, and other worse-than-perspiration side effects. A treatment called iontophoresis, which involves immersing your hands and feet in water charged with a low-voltage electrical current, has a good track record.

In extreme cases, people turn to surgery. Underarm sweat glands are removed using liposuction, scraped away (a technique called curettage), or sliced out along with a swatch of skin. The most drastic surgical intervention is endoscopic thoracic sympathectomy, in which the nerves that control sweat are cut, cauterized, or clamped. The results are immediate, but the possible complications include increased sweating in other areas of the body.

Then there's the drug made famous for smoothing famous faces: Botox. In 2004, the FDA approved the use of Botox injections to treat severe underarm sweating (by blocking the release of sweat-triggering acetylcholine). Pending approval of other treatment sites, many doctors now use Botox to treat palmar sweating as well. Dave Respess, a 35-year-old former police officer, is a believer. Concerned that sweat was interfering with his current job as a driving instructor training soldiers to maneuver through the streets of Baghdad, Respess tried Drysol and iontophoresis with no luck. Then he opted for Botox injections in his palms and fingertips. Within five days, his palms dried up. "I'm able to control the steering wheel a lot better," he says. "It's had such a tremendous impact on my life. Not just professionally, but socially."

Respess says the results last for about four to five months, at which point he needs more injections—and they hurt. "It's pretty painful," he says. "But I'll go through 15 minutes of pain to get five months of comfort. It's worth it."

Back in the sweatbox, things are warming up. I can feel the first tingle of the perspiration glands letting go in certain areas of my body. I know this feeling. Once you feel the tingle, there is no going back. By the time Dr. Fealey orders me removed 30 minutes later, I look, well, disturbing. My glistening violet skin gives me the appearance of a burnt, bruised, and greasy plum.

If your life is being soured by sweat, you can find help without turning purple. Start by contacting a specialist in hyperhidrosis. (The IHHS has a searchable database at sweathelp.org.) The doctor may measure the diameter of your pit stains (more than 20 centimeters may indicate problem perspiration) and read your palms (sweat that reaches your fingertips can be a sign of severe hyperhidrosis). Some doctors use a TST to rule out more serious medical problems, which is why I'm a little nervous to hear my own results.

"You have mild primary focal hyperhidrosis—emotional sweating confined to areas like the palms, feet, or armpits," says Dr. Fealey. "We categorize you as such because your palms and the soles of your feet showed some sweating before you got in the heat. And then, of course, you showed a nice response to the mental arithmetic."

So I'm officially sorta sweaty. I don't need Botox so much as I need to keep track of my phone and stop buying nose-hair clippers along with my rutabagas. On the upside, should I ever find myself incarcerated with a large man called Sally, he will find me nearly impossible to hold.

2007

P.S. A decade later, I'm embarrassed by that last line. It's cheesy, clichéd, uninformed, and unfunny. I was gonna cut it for this edition, but that'd be a copout.

MIKE EATS BEANS

I am about to ignore the advice of my doctor. Again. Really, he deserves better. Randall Casper, MD, is a gentle, matter-of-fact fellow who has been our trusted family physician since the day he saved my grandfather's life by making a diagnosis other docs had missed. For years he has treated me with professionalism and patience, and now I am about to walk out of the examination room and leave his prescription on the desk.

Like millions of other American men, I have high cholesterol. When I had my levels checked for the first time seven years ago, my HDL (good) cholesterol was a healthy 50 milligrams per deciliter (mg/dl), but my LDL (bad) cholesterol was 142 mg/dl—borderline high, according to the American Heart Association. I told Dr. Casper I would improve my diet and I resolved to eat nothing but alfalfa sprouts and apple wedges from that day forward.

Nineteen months later, my LDL had climbed to 151 mg/dl. "I know you're trying to eat better," said Dr. Casper, kindly ignoring all evidence to the contrary, "but this is really reaching the point where you should consider a cholesterol-lowering medication." I crossed my heart and swore this time I'd kick the Little Debbie cakes forever. Then I avoided having my cholesterol checked for another three and a half years.

Now I'm back in his office.

It's not good.

"Your LDL cholesterol is up to 175," he says. Jiminy. All my celery-stick promises, down a greasy drain.

Dr. Casper raises his gaze, and I feel a little prickle of embarrassment. After a pair of second chances, I'm the kid who brought home his third bad report card, and we both know what's coming next. "I really think you need to start on a statin," he says. The prescription pad is right there on the table. He's toying with the pen in his pocket.

I say I'll get back to him.

If you buy most of the headlines and all of the advertisements, only a suicidal chucklehead would dawdle at the opportunity to outlive his forebears by popping one of today's cholesterol-smashing miracle pills. Since their introduction in 1987, statins—drugs that block cholesterol production in the liver—have garnered rave reviews. And improved cholesterol scores are only part of the story. Lately, claims are being made regarding the ability of statins to prevent cancer, fortify bones, and strengthen erections. A recent article in the journal *Clinical Infectious Diseases* suggests that statins may even be used as a weapon to ward off a global influenza pandemic. So what's holding me back?

In 2001, a statin marketed under the name Baycol was pulled from pharmacy shelves after being associated with rhabdomyolysis—a muscle-wasting condition in which toxic by-products from muscle fragments enter the bloodstream and clog the kidneys, potentially causing organ failure and eventual death. Five years later the National Lipid Association's statin-safety task force put the odds of muscle-related side effects from the current crop of statins at 1 in 20,000. But researchers suggest that intense training, such as for a marathon, may bump the number up. Some scientists have also questioned whether statin-associated spikes in blood levels of liver enzymes indicate trouble in the organ, and there is ongoing debate about the drugs causing memory loss.

While experts warn of understated risks, a growing number suggest that the benefits are equally overstated. A recent article in *Businessweek* cited aggressive drug company marketing that employs tricky statistics (one statin ad boasted a 36 percent reduction in the risk of a heart attack even though the drug was only slightly more effective than a placebo). "If you've already had a heart attack, taking a statin has a small but very real effect," says Jerome Hoffman, MD, a professor of clinical medicine at UCLA. "But you'd need at least 50 people to take it for five years for one of them to benefit. Yet all will incur great costs for the drugs and the doctor visits, and will worry and risk side effects."

I reside just inside the skeptic's camp, although my reservations are based as much on finances and stubborn pride as on the medical research. And then there's my wife.

I have married a strong and willful woman, and she does not want me on the pill. It's tough to argue with her: She's strikingly beautiful and has a master's degree. I have one eyebrow and a bachelor's. Because my degree is in nursing and I have spent nearly 20 years as an EMT and firefighter doing CPR on people whose high cholesterol has caught up with them, I tend to welcome the help of Western medicine. My wife, on the other hand, spent her postgraduate years in the company of shamans, yogis, assorted hempen types, and lately, a home-schooled nutritionist. The nutritionist has her convinced that I can beat high cholesterol simply by fine-tuning my diet. In short, she wants me to load up on beans and fish oil.

She says the particular type of soluble fiber in beans (which is also in oats and barley) reduces the absorption of dietary cholesterol by sponging up excess intestinal bile. Since our livers draw LDL cholesterol from the bloodstream to manufacture fresh bile and replenish the supply, the more bile that's removed by the fiber, the more cholesterol will fall. As for the fish oil, it contains omega-3 fatty acids, which have been shown to lower triglycerides.

I trust Dr. Casper. But I do not have to sleep with him. I'm going to give the beans a shot.

◆ ◆ ◆

For the first couple of months, my wife feeds me beans twice a day, buying lentils from the local food co-op in such quantities that we now qualify for the commune rate. I reduce my intake of cookies and quickie-mart doughnuts and consume more fresh fruit. (A National Heart, Lung, and Blood Institute study found that eating more fruit and vegetables may keep LDL cholesterol low.) Between meals I try to snack on palmfuls of dried fruit and nuts rather than oh, say, the usual quarter pound of chocolate chips and bowl of Lucky Charms. At bedtime, when I remember, I swallow a few fish-oil capsules.

And that's pretty much it. Hardly rigorous. After four months, I have myself tested and the results are surprising. My LDL has dropped from 175 to 152—still too high, but an appreciable decline. My triglycerides are relatively unchanged at 86, but anything below 150 is normal. The only negative? My HDL has fallen to 39, and the AHA maintains that an HDL below 40 puts me at major risk for heart disease.

But the progress is significant enough that I decide to expand my "dietary portfolio." That's a phrase I came across in a 2006 study published in the *American Journal of Clinical Nutrition.* Just as a diversified stock portfolio yields more reliable results over the long term, a diversified dietary portfolio can pay off with life-extending dividends. It combines foods high in soluble fiber (yep, beans), nuts (they can lower LDL cholesterol and help improve HDL and triglycerides), soy protein (it reduces LDL), and plant sterols (compounds that block cholesterol absorption).

"Each of these foods can lower cholesterol about 5 percent," says Cyril Kendall, PhD, a research scientist at the University of Toronto who helped develop the dietary-portfolio concept. "By putting them all in the same diet, you produce an additive effect resulting in about a 20 percent reduction." Limit your intake of saturated fat and dietary cholesterol, and you subtract another 10 percent. The total payoff: Some people in Kendall's studies saw their cholesterol drop, on average, 25 to 35 percent, a reduction similar to that produced by some statins.

• • •

My day begins with oatmeal.

To complement the soluble fiber, I stir in my daily allotment of nuts and dried fruit and crown it all with a dollop of Promise Activ, a margarine-like spread laced with plant sterols. I eat fish two or three times a week (for traveling, I slip foil pouches of tuna into my briefcase), and barring that, I pop fish-oil capsules. I have an occasional steak but stick mostly to venison because it's leaner and my freezer is packed with it. Apart from a tofu stir-fry now and then, I try to avoid soy out of concern for its possible estrogenic effects on men and the fact that soy milk makes me heave.

When I'm jonesing for sweets, I go for red grapefruit. A 2006 study conducted in Israel found that people who ate one red grapefruit a day saw a drop in their cholesterol and triglyceride levels. Anyone who already takes a statin should skip this tip— grapefruit can compound the drug's negative effects.

A 2005 review of HDL-management strategies in the *New England Journal of Medicine* identified physical activity and weight loss as primary methods of raising HDL cholesterol, so I run four times a week and try to limit my food portions—not easy for a man raised by lard-slinging farm wives and doting Scandinavian aunties who view overeating as a profound expression of love.

Most importantly, whatever I have for lunch or supper I eat with a side of legumes—half a cup, minimum. Got to have that fiber. If worse comes to worse, I binge on Metamucil. That's right. My diet has a gimmick. A secret weapon. It's the bedtime snack of octogenarians everywhere, but I'm going to make it cool again.

For the first week or so, I took the powder. It's really not that bad. Then one evening I went a little lean on the water, and it was like choking down orange-flavored squid guts. I switched to the capsules. You just wash them down and forget about them. Or forget about them for roughly 12 hours, at which point you literally flush the cholesterol from your system. I really don't like to discuss this sort of thing, but I set some personal records.

Five months after my last blood test, it's time to check again. I'd peg my compliance with the dietary portfolio at 70 to 80 percent, and I wonder if it will be enough.

Wow, is it ever. LDL cholesterol: 120, down from 175. Triglycerides, 63. And the addition of running has helped bump my HDL up from 39 to 45.

I'm thrilled. It was so much easier than I'd anticipated. I was never miserable. I had to exercise self-control, but it wasn't draconian. Sometimes I forgot my grapefruit, and sometimes I found myself on the road with no sterol spread. Occasionally, I caved and had doughnuts or went up the street to TJ's for a Tubby Burger and fries, and still the numbers came around.

"It's a real-world approach," says Kendall. "We all try to behave ourselves, but every so often there are dinners, you're traveling, you just have a craving . . . if you can enjoy yourself once in a while and still achieve those sorts of reductions, that's terrific."

Still, Dr. Casper has seen this before. "I've had patients lower their cholesterol dramatically just by improving their diets," he says. "The trouble is, the next time I see them, the results are back where they were. It's one thing to move the numbers down—it's quite another to maintain them."

So I come out and ask him: "What are the odds I can keep my cholesterol at these levels without using a statin?" He's quiet for a while. "I don't have any scientific data to answer that," he says finally. "But I have 21 years of frontline experience and I think your chances are probably less than fifty-fifty."

He chuckles. "And I'm trying to be kind!"

• • •

If a year passes and I backslide, perhaps I'll ask for that prescription. But in our obsession with miracle pills we sometimes forget you can pull off the same fabulous feat equipped with nothing but your own body and a grocery cart. There's your miracle. You should have seen my wife's face light up when I laid these latest numbers on her. Lucky one-eyebrowed me: I have a woman who thinks low cholesterol is sexy.

2008

P.S. My daily dietary habits remain a train wreck, especially when I'm on the road or up late writing, which accounts for the greater portion of my life. But every day I eat them beans.

MIKE GOES METROSEXUAL

Remember the term "metrosexual"? It popped up in the mid-1990s and referred to a man who was very meticulous about appearance. Naturally, I'd be the guy you'd want to write about that. Also, before you read this, you might need to refresh your memory via Wikipedia regarding Paris Hilton. The person, not the French hotel.

Today I will have the first manicure of my life and I want it to go well—which is why I am scrubbing the dried blood from my cuticles. Two days ago I was elbow-deep in deer guts. A crust of dehydrated corpuscles remain lodged in the crevices bordering each nail bed. I towel off and inspect each hand beneath the bathroom light, then have a look at my face in the mirror. After a week spent tromping the swamps of northern Wisconsin in search of freezer meat, I am shaggy and windburned and smell vaguely of Tink's Original #69 Doe-in-Rut Buck Lure. But not for long. I have been airlifted to Manhattan for a three-day whirlwind of rejuvenation and pampering including procedures not easily explained to the well-armed fellows of hunting camp.

I know what you're thinking, but the term *metrosexual* is so last deer season. These days the men's grooming industry is betting the farm on Regular Joe. "Over time it has become much less taboo for men of all walks of life and parts of the country to use these products," says Tony Sosnick of Anthony Logistics, a company that produces grooming products specifically designed for men. "Slowly but surely skin care is making its way to the places where it ordinarily hasn't been." And so, as a guy whose idea of skin care amounts to turning my face toward the shower head, I am turning myself over to the professionals on behalf of Regular Joes everywhere.

SHAVE

Things get off to a bad start when Master Barber Ely Mirzakandov seats me in one of the two barber chairs at the Art of Shaving at 373 Madison Avenue and presses a folded linen cloth to my forehead. I am so primed for a week of herbal wraps and healing salts and Native American flute music that I assume Mirzakandov is performing some Zen-based pre-shave centering ritual. I sit up straight, giving gentle resistance to the pressure of his hand, and feel his power flow through my brow. Then he mutters something, and I realize he is simply trying to get me to recline against the headrest.

Mirzakandov, a taciturn fellow who looks more suited to shaving old-school bankers than aromatic dandies, shears my deer hunting beard with clippers before cinching my head into a moist towel heated right to the edge of comfort. It is quiet and steamy inside the towel, and the angle of the chair relaxes me until I remember this is how they got Albert Anastasia back in '57. But when the towels come off and I feel the cool air against my eyelids, all I see is Mirzakandov standing ready with a palmful of heated shaving cream. The cream came purling from a whirring dispenser, and it smooths across my cheek as warm and weightless as the breath of a woman. Canned shaving cream is spackle by comparison, although you can improve your home shaving experience by dunking the can in warm water while you bathe.

This is my first straight razor shave, and I get a primal tingle at the feel of the steel against my neck. When the razor passes over my carotid, I can't help but think of chickens (and worse). After the first pass, Mirzakandov wraps me in more hot towels and repeats the process. On the second pass, the scraping is more refined. It is a pleasure to feel him working across the point of my chin, a spot my safety razor never seems to get quite right. When he blades along the side of my neck, he presses down on the corresponding shoulder, a simple move that tightens the skin and eases passage of the razor. His entire routine is filled with moves of economy and grace. Later, when I find a mirror, I check all the tricky spots—including those sneaky whiskers in the nostril crease—and Mirzakandov got them all. What's more, the following morning, my face is still smooth.

HAIRCUT

When I arrive at Paul Labrecque Salon & Spa for my appointment for a haircut by Martial Vivot, I draw on my experience as the former boyfriend of a French farm girl and ask to see *"Mar-see-ahl."* The receptionist looks up as if I have escargot dangling from each nostril, and says, "You are here to see *Marshal?*" To be fair, I am wearing Ragged Glory jeans and smell of Wal-Mart. She points me upstairs, where I sit between two women dressed in a fashion that reminds me of platinum and spankings. They are catlike and fragrant. I, on the other hand, feel like a perverted orangutan wedged between two Fabergé eggs and quickly lurch away to lurk in the hall until an assistant hands me a brown robe and ushers me to Martial's barber chair.

Martial is renowned as a genius with the shears, and he is wearing a suit the cut of which says *you could never pull this off,* but he is very friendly. I feel bad that I don't have much to offer him. I am not bald yet, but I am Bald Man Walking. Martial circles my large round cranium with the ease of a *danseur,* his scissors flashing *snickety-snick-snick-snickety,* and when he pauses to step back with the blades poised in midair to regard his progress, I think, poor man, this is like asking Clapton to play air guitar. "If you are balding, you should avoid sharp lines. Go for more shading," he says, gauging the light off my dome. "Lightening your hair is also helpful." Martial catches my eye in the mirror, fluffs his own lightened and waning strands, and grins. "Short is good too," he says, revving his scissors and returning to my scalp, "but you should tan first." I see why: The top of my head resembles an ostrich egg with bristles.

When Martial finishes miming my haircut, he swivels me around and stares hard at my unibrow. All my life I have stubbornly refused to pluck, shave, or otherwise establish a false median between the brows and the bridge of my nose. For the purposes of this story, I have agreed to have it waxed. Martial has other ideas. "I think we will not wax them," he says (it is sweet of him to use the term "them"). "Waxing is quick, but it can create a harsh line. I think we should tweeze."

"Jill!"

THE TWEEZING

Eyebrow specialist Jill has a bright smile, a sunny demeanor, and a voracious pair of tweezers. "You might want to close your eyes," she chirps, as I recline. She forgot to add, ". . . *and bite down hard on a whiskey-soaked rag.*" Jill's tweezer-speed is blinding, and the pain is breathtaking. My heart races, my palms go cold, and good Lord, my *ears ache.* As a tear pops out of my eye and runs into my aching ear, Jill trills, "I recommend that my clients take an Advil first . . . or a martini!" By the time she is finished "shaping" my eyebrows, I am weeping like Jimmy Swaggart dicing onions. Jill tips me up and even through the watery blur I can see two distinct eyebrows. I also have blotchy port wine stains where my eyebrows used to join—if you're getting "shaped" for a special day, make your appointment a day or two prior. And take that Advil. Or a jello shot.

SCALP MASSAGE

When someone jerks out your eyebrow hairs, just having them cease and desist is a spa in itself, but when Pirkko Vaisanen, director of Labrecque's Hair and Scalp Repair Division, drapes a heated aromatherapy collar around my neck and begins gently scrubbing my scalp with the bristles of a hairbrush, it feels so good I could shake my leg like a dog. Vaisanen has the perfect voice for her job, soothing and placid. I couldn't pick her out of a lineup, but I remember her voice, soft and strong as she urged me to close my eyes and succumb to the sensation of her 45-minute scalp treatment. "You must care for the scalp, because the scalp skin is part of the face," says Vaisanen. My treatment includes an exfoliating eucalyptus cream, essential oils, hot towel wraps, and something Vaisanen calls the "Indian Head" massage, which is purported to unknot blockages, drain away toxins, and calm the spirit. When she finishes, I'm not any prettier, and I can't testify to the blockages and toxins, but my spirit is the consistency of warm butterscotch.

Before I leave, Vaisanen shares her home remedy for dry, brittle hair. As a nearly bald teetotaler, I haven't been able to test it, but you'll be pleased to know it involves beer—two ounces mixed with one ounce of water and three drops of lemon essential oil. Vaisanen recommends you massage it into your scalp and leave it for one hour, which should give you just enough time to drink the rest of the six-pack before getting your eyebrows shaped.

FACIAL

Pity Anna Augustsson, because she is looking at my face through an illuminated magnifying glass and squeezing blackheads that must appear to be the size of lard tubs. My nose wrinkles just thinking of it. "I have had some guys say, 'What are you doing?!?' and jump off the table," says Augustsson, a friendly, energetic woman who is employed as an aesthetician at Nickel Spa in Chelsea. Aestheticians call this process "extraction," and it is also available for your back.

It takes about five minutes to complete my extractions. "You had some clogging, but nothing unusual," said Augustsson. My facial skin tends to be more oily than dry, and the clogging often leads to pimples. "Witch hazel can be a great off-the-shelf way to clean and tone those oily areas," says Augustsson, as she switches off the magnifier and begins to give me a hydrating facial. The small room has become cozy and dark, and ambient New Age music is playing in the background. After swabbing my cheeks with an unidentified potion, she thrums her finger pads across my face like a gang of Riverdancing Thumbelinas. It feels so good I can feel my ears wilt. When she finishes I am unable to form a complete sentence and am thus spared the humiliation of begging for more.

PEDICURE AND MANICURE

My only previous pedicure experience came from helping my father trim sheep hooves. It was smelly, sweaty work, but at least the sheep had the good grace not to giggle—unlike me, tittering like a three-year-old at a tea party while Irina, the aesthetician at Nickel Spa, rubs lotion on my feet, looks up, and says, "Ticklish?" I feel weirdly vulnerable in the elevated chair with my jeans cuffed up to reveal my naked white toes. When Irina gently towels my feet it's like Huck Finn meets Mary Magdalene. When she keeps repositioning my foot because I don't know how to hold it, I feel like a dumb draft horse bucking a petite blacksmith.

But Irina is fearless, going into the dreadful corners of my toes to clip the nails and clear all extraneous goodies, trim back the cuticles, and scrub away calluses. It takes her three tries to trim the nail on my little toe because every time she touches it I twitch. After wrestling my foot into submission, she clips the nail. Each nail is then filed and buffed. I decline the polish and luxuriate in a final foot rub, and try not to squirm. Poor Irina. It's like a day at the toe rodeo.

After I put my boots and socks back on, Irina swivels my chair to face the manicure table. My nails are fairly short, so Irina just files and buffs them. While she is inspecting and trimming my cuticles, and then moisturizing and massaging each hand, I am thinking I am a long way from the deer hunting swamps of Wisconsin. And as I sit with my fingers delicately extended beneath the warm, whirring air of the nail polish dryer, I am thinking it's a long way back . . .

TOPPING IT OFF WITH A TAN

If Paris Hilton has taught me anything, it is that all the languorous fine-tuning in the world is for naught if you don't top it off with a spray tan. And so I have been whisked away by Town Car to a tanning emporium, where I am standing naked with Vaseline on my toenails, facing what appears to be an upended maroon Jacuzzi studded with spray jets reminiscent of the booths my auto shop buddies back home use to repaint truck fenders. There is Vaseline on my fingernails as well, to prevent staining. The very tan, tall, thick-haired man who led me back here has given me anatomically detailed instructions on how to position my body so that all crevices and portions get coverage. I am told to hold my eyes closed or my eyelids will flash white every time I blink. He also showed me a sort of shower cap designed to protect my hairline from overspray, then he glanced at my head and said, "You won't need that."

So I am stripped and alone now, doing a quick mental run-through of the tanning tai chi, knowing that once I hit the button I will have a limited number of passes to get it right. The jets come on and off in sequence, starting at my top and heading for my, well, *bottom*. I do the tan-dance, which is reminiscent of Steve Martin doing "King Tut" on that old *Saturday Night Live* episode. The spray is toxic and sweet smelling all at once, and as it comes blowing out of the jets I twist and turn—*funky Tut!*—close my eyes, and dream of Paris.

When the final spritz spritzes, I emerge from the rusty fog, hurriedly wipe myself down, notice there are bronzer clumps up in my underarm hair, toss my clothes on and run to the waiting car feeling vaguely naughty and a bit sticky. Back in the hotel mirror, I definitely have a healthier hue, but I messed up on the Vaseline and now have a pair of orange toenails.

SUMMARY

Back home, they noticed the tan, of course. The eyebrows didn't attract as much attention as I thought they would. My wife approved, but most people didn't notice unless I pointed them out, and then they'd say, "I *thought* something was different!" I quite happily let them grow back in. No more shaping, but I do keep them trimmed. Jill—she of the tweezers—warns men not to cut their eyebrows too short. "They'll bristle and stick out," she says. I trim them just enough so that I can see through my rifle scope.

I've been doing my own extractions, thank you, but I just peer in the mirror and squeeze, and there is no question a professional aesthetician does a better job. After my visit with Anna, the breakouts all but stop. One of the more unexpected benefits of my professional grooming experience comes from my pedicure, of all things. All my life I have read that you should cut your toenails squarely, and I never have. As a result I have had intermittent problems with my big toenails getting sore and sometimes ingrown. After Irina reshaped them, the problems disappeared, and I have carefully maintained them in the pattern she established. It will be a while before I trim away the final strip of orange tanner.

I haven't had another facial, but I have had several hourlong massages. One of the unifying elements of my entire grooming experience was how each procedure involved stillness and surrender of control. For better or worse, I am highly unlikely to change my clodhopping ways and dive into a life of scrubs and pedicures, but the good news for the male grooming industry is that I am not impervious to the appeal of aesthetics. A full-on straight razor shave will remain a rare treat (I once cut off the end of my little finger while making a sandwich, so buying my own straight razor is out of the question), but because of the experience I have altered my shaving routine. I've ditched the aerosol can and take an extra minute to prepare my face with a glycerin cleansing soap (the citrus bar by Anthony Logistics For Men is my favorite . . . it smells like tangerines and tea) and then apply a shave cream that goes on light and thin. After trying several, I went with Anthony Logistics again—although it says "fragrance-free" on the plain gray-and-white squeeze tube, the cream has a mild eucalyptus scent. This one-two combination has changed my shaving experience from a tortuous scrape to a smooth, refreshing mini-spa moment. I also keep a little face moisturizer handy—not because I think it will make me beautiful, but because it feels healthy, and by keeping an exfoliant in the shower where I'm reminded to use it intermittently, I've noticed some improvement in the pimple-prone problem areas of my face. And I now brush my bald head regularly to keep the blood circulating and because it feels good.

There are, of course, limits. I am no longer wearing nail polish, and I don't miss the aromatherapy, although I am seeking investment capital for the creation of a line of heated camo-print aromatherapy collars that give off the scent of Tink's #69. And I'll never set foot in a tanning booth again unless I'm asked to go deer hunting with Paris Hilton.

EARLY 2000s

P.S. Remember earlier we talked about "kill fees"? This piece got one. The magazine's fashion editor felt I didn't take the topic seriously enough. He was probably right on, although I still take pretty good care of my toenails.

POISON IVY *WHERE?*

Outside Magazine asked 13 writers to describe the greatest calamity they'd ever faced in the wild. There were stories of avalanches, 60-foot waves, and guerrilla-war gunfire. All I can say is, everything is relative.

I learned to defecate in the woods while I was still in single digits. Our small Wisconsin farm was surrounded by hundreds of acres of swamp and forest, and my siblings and I were often out of washroom range when the urge struck. We became precocious connoisseurs of organic cleansing media. Wipeability factors varied: Oak leaves gave good coverage, but their slickness limited absorption. Pine needles were worthless, even injurious, but had the benefit of smelling like tree-shaped air fresheners. Moss was fragile, soggy, and sandy, but it had a decent swab factor. Finally, I can say without reservation that a fat handful of poison ivy leaves did the job quite nicely. The initial job, that is. The sequelae, to use a physician's term, were untenable.

I was 14, which, given my experience toileting alfresco, made my mistake doubly knot-headed. Grandpa had taken a passel of us to a riverside swimming hole. I still remember squatting in the bushes before jumping in, prospecting for leaves after it was too late to relocate. The only trees within reach were pines. I groped behind me and felt a clump of flat, wide leaves. Bingo!

It took a while for the itching to commence. Early on, while still in the water, I felt squirmy twinges of an intimate nature, but, hey, what's new? Back home two hours later, I was racewalking around the living room, fully prepared to drop my shorts and do the naughty-puppy carpet scoot. Cross-eyed and panting, I racked my brain and reviewed the day. When I got around to reenacting the outdoor toity session, I blanched.

I wound up with such a blistering case that I was taken to a clinic for corticosteroid shots. The doctor also prescribed a topical cream and instructed my mother (a nurse) to apply it daily. Florence Nightingale herself wouldn't have shown up for that gig. I spent a week sleeping on my stomach, fitful and straddle-legged. Standard bathroom procedure went out the window, replaced by a wincing gavotte in which I lowered myself to the seat, did the deed, drew a baking soda bath, and delicately cleansed and patted myself dry. One misstep and I would collapse into a seizure of spastic monkey-scratching. Years later I came across a poster in a print shop that said IT'S NOT THE BURNING, IT'S THE ITCHING, MAN! and I thought, Amen.

For a long time, the fact that I'd wiped my butt with poison ivy was my little secret. I have to believe Mom had her suspicions, even though I explained it away by saying I'd backed into the stuff while changing into my bathing suit. She kept a log of my childhood illnesses, and the entry for August 7, 1979, says, "poison ivy, lower trunk." Delicately put, don't you think?

2005

THAT EARS RINGING THING

I am no logger (just ask my brother the logger), but we heat our house with a woodstove, and I do like to run a chain saw. So I was happy in the forest a few months ago as I revved the engine, dropping trees and bucking them into firewood length for next winter. The snarling roar of the saw rose and fell, safely muffled by my hearing protectors.

Then the saw coughed, and died. Outta gas.

The forest fell silent. But my head? Not so much. The moment the engine noise ceased, my noggin filled with a high-tensile squeal. The sound seemed to pass through my brain, from ear to ear, like the thinnest steel guitar string drawn so taut that it seems about to snap—and yet never does.

As quickly as I could, I laid the saw down on the ground and shucked the earmuffs. The squeal didn't stop but it faded, and it no longer felt as if someone was shooting a laser beam through my skull.

My cranium used to be quiet. Then 15 years ago, I pulled an all-nighter in a recording studio while wearing a pair of headphones cranked blisteringly high. When I stepped outside at dawn, my ears were making Charlie Brown wah-wah sounds. Within 48 hours, the wah-wah stopped but a ringing sound remained. I was worried: Had I damaged my ears?

I made an appointment with an audiologist. Surprisingly, my

hearing checked out fine, but the ringing wouldn't quit. "It's tinnitus," said the audiologist. "Some people hear buzzing or chirping. It might just go away," she said. "Or not."

It did not go away. It kept me awake at night. The more I tried to ignore it, the more it bothered me. And it didn't just bother me—it made me feel ashamed and guilty. Like it was a signal broadcasting the same unceasing message: You wrecked your ears, you idiot. I was depressed. I couldn't sleep. Most of all, I felt dumb for being this upset about a sound.

I wanted help, so I started researching treatment options, contacting tinnitus experts, and learning everything I could about the affliction. When you begin delving into tinnitus, you quickly discover two camps: those who say TIN-it-us, and those who say t'NIGHT-us. And good luck getting even the experts to agree. But however you pronounce it, the American Tinnitus Association says more than 45 million Americans have the condition. Some 16 million find it bothersome enough to seek treatment, and 2 million report it to be extreme and sometimes so overwhelming that they can't function normally on a day-to-day basis. It's more common among men than women—perhaps because men are more likely to be employed in noisy jobs. Emergency service personnel, such as firefighters and medical responders, and members of the US military—especially combat veterans—are at higher risk.

By the time I'd gathered all that information, several weeks had passed, and something odd had happened: My tinnitus no longer bothered me. Oh, it was still there, and I still didn't like it, but it had receded into the background. My depression and insomnia were gone.

Later—much later—I would discover that the timing of these changes was no coincidence.

But for the time being, I decided that I could probably live with my tinnitus.

◆ ◆ ◆

Before you try to live with tinnitus, find out from your doctor if you even have to. "Most cases can't be treated with medicine or surgery," says James W. Hall III, PhD, a professor at the Osborne College of Audiology at Salus University in Pennsylvania, "but it's always important to identify the few people who can be helped by a physician, because tinnitus might be a symptom of ear or neurological diseases that sometimes are very serious."

He's primarily talking about tumor-triggered tinnitus as well as the kind caused by cardiovascular disease. But the nonstop noise can also be brought on by Lyme disease, jaw misalignment, and ototoxicity, i.e., as a side effect of medications including aspirin and certain antibiotics. And you know the expression "I got my bell rung"? If it keeps ringing, get checked out for a concussion, as tinnitus is a common consequence of a bad bonk.

In most situations, however, tinnitus occurs as a result of damage to the ear from too much noise exposure for too long and too often.

But what's funny about the condition (except to sufferers like myself) is that it truly is all in a person's head. If someone could stick a microphone inside my skull, they wouldn't hear the ringing. That's because my brain, primarily the auditory cortex, is generating only the perception of noise. In some cases, this is an attempt by the cortex to replace a frequency range that can no longer be detected due to damaged hearing. Researchers have identified some of the mechanisms underlying tinnitus perception, but unfortunately, just as often there's no explanation for why it creates these phantom sounds. That's why tinnitus is so difficult to treat, leaving those afflicted with few options and sometimes even less hope.

When Austin musician Mark Stancato wound up with a career-derailing case of tinnitus in 2013 and was told by two separate physicians that nothing could be done, he became so desperate that he considered suicide. "I remember driving home past this gun store and having visions of buying a gun, going home, writing a note, and putting the pistol to my head," says Stancato.

Frightened, he sought help from a psychiatrist, who treated him with counseling and antianxiety medications. "Now I'm back at a place where it's manageable," says Stancato, who has since returned to performing. "Sometimes I can't hear it at all." But he says he'll never forget the time he was begging an otolaryngologist for help, and the doc replied, "Well, tinnitus never killed anybody." "That isn't true," says Stancato, and he's right: He got out alive, but a 2014 report by the American Academy of Otolaryngology cites suicide as a special concern when tinnitus is accompanied by psychological issues.

Recently I noticed that my tinnitus seemed to have cranked up again. I had taken to using little tricks to keep it at bay—placing my smartphone beneath my pillow at night to play white-noise apps, or sleeping with a fan running—anything to drown out the ringing. But in quiet moments it felt more pervasive, and if I popped in earplugs, it was disturbingly distracting. Now and then—especially if I was anxious or depressed—the ringing would increase, and behind it I'd hear that voice from way back: Your ears . . . they're getting worse . . .

I recalled my first go-round with tinnitus, and how the more I learned about it—the more I faced it—the less it troubled me. And I realized that it was time to stare it down again.

I went to NYU Langone Medical Center for testing. During the exam, audiologist Theresa Shaw, AuD, filled my headphones with beeps, hisses, and high-frequency squeals. The verdict? "Your hearing is actually quite good," said Dr. Shaw. Whether or not my tinnitus had gotten worse was more difficult to tell, but she said that was beside the point.

"Whether the sound you are hearing is measurable in an objective way is essentially irrelevant in terms of treatment," said Dr. Shaw. "Your body is experiencing it. Your body and your mind. There is a link between tinnitus and the limbic system, hooking us into that fight-or-flight response. And then it's the chicken or the egg . . . the tinnitus may exacerbate the fight-or-flight response, the fight-or-flight response creates more of a focus on tinnitus, and so on."

Even among experts, there is no universal endorsement of any one best way to disrupt the cycle. Some people find relief through simple interventions like hearing aids or sound generators. A rare few others require something more drastic, like cochlear implants that provide electrical stimulation to the auditory nerves. Some experience relief using alternative treatments like ginkgo biloba or acupuncture. But most experts agree that tinnitus should be treated using a three-pronged approach: audiological, neurological, and psychological.

Audiological treatment includes assessing and treating any hearing loss. The neurological component involves the use of sound to either distract from the tinnitus or retrain the brain into perceiving the tinnitus as diminished. The psychological component focuses not on eliminating the tinnitus but on reducing the reaction to it, as well as not compulsively focusing on it.

"When a patient tells me, 'I still have tinnitus; I just don't care about it anymore,' that's a victory," said Shaw.

A week later, I attended a two-day yoga and meditation retreat with my wife. While she has been studying, practicing, and teaching yoga for years, I wouldn't know a downward dog from an upward squirrel. My morning meditation routine consists of tapping my foot impatiently as the coffee beans grind.

The retreat began with an introductory lecture from a yogi, and then we closed our eyes as he led us into our first meditation.

"We must find ourselves before we can fix ourselves," the yogi said. I rolled my closed eyes but resolved to give it a try. The room was silent. Too silent, because with no background noise, my tinnitus took over, whining its way into my consciousness, crowding everything else out. I tried to ignore it and—assuming meditation requires soft, beautiful things—conjured up a flower.

The tinnitus laser beam incinerated it.

The yogi spoke, softly. "Whatever enters your consciousness can be the focus."

Whatever that means, I thought. The tinnitus came zinging back, like a stainless-steel bee.

The yogi spoke again: "Meditation is not about blocking every distraction but rather choosing one distraction and examining it."

And right then I stopped my snarky inner monologue. Rather than trying to ignore the tinnitus, or push it away, or distract myself, I homed right in on it. Tried to hear every note of it. Tried to imagine what it would look like on an oscilloscope. Gave it my deepest attention, as if it were the most beautiful song ever played.

And something weird happened: The tinnitus faded, like someone turned down the volume.

My wife and the yogi may have led me to the future of tinnitus treatment. In a Duke University study, patients who were extremely handicapped by their tinnitus reported relief after adding therapies like meditation to standard treatments. And a 2015 UC San Francisco pilot study found that patients experienced a clinically significant decrease in the perceived annoyance and perception of tinnitus after attending a mindfulness-based meditation program. They had focused on their tinnitus with "curiosity" rather than trying to banish it.

None of these researchers are claiming cure, though I wish they were. I'd love to drift off to sleep to the sound of silence rather than the sound of whatever's playing under my pillow. I'd love to kill the chain saw and hear nothing but . . . nothing. No, my tinnitus (I'm a TIN-it-us guy, by the way) is here to stay. But the more I meditate on it—as opposed to obsessing—the more I hear the ringing for just what it is: the perfect shrieking path to inner peace.

2015

TEETOTAL

Dinner was finished, and the party had begun. My host reached into a cabinet above the refrigerator to draw forth a dark bottle filled with an elixir that was completely legal, available without prescription, and—most researchers agree—would provide me with a longer, healthier life. It also goes great with rare steak and fine cheese.

He poured and offered. Drink up, the studies said, and I would show up for work more often, be less likely to have a heart attack (and more likely to survive one if I did), decrease my odds of developing dementia, and perhaps even avoid the dreaded common cold.

I looked at the glass. Good red wine.

"No thanks," I said.

I have never had a beer. Or a shot. Or a glass of wine. I did chug some high-octane cough syrup when I was a tot. (Mom kept a bottle of stuff that tasted like crushed pine needles.) And once, in my youth, after digging the last spoonful of chocolate syrup out of an ice cream cup at a wedding reception, I was surprised to find that it tasted bitter. I sat there for a second with my head tilted quizzically, only to realize as it slid down my gullet that I had just ingested demon rum. So perhaps I can't claim to be a *total* teetotaler, but those few teaspoons represent the lifelong sum of my recreational boozing.

Whenever someone offers me a drink and I decline, they invariably react in one of two ways. They either back away with eyes wide and hands spread in a "no harm, no foul" stance, saying, "Okay, that's cool, no worries," clearly thinking they're about to receive a temperance lecture, or, more commonly, the person pauses, and then—as the false realization dawns—says, "Ohhh," and surreptitiously slides his own drink out of sight while giving a meaningful nod to acknowledge my struggle for sobriety.

Truth is, I just don't drink.

But lately I've been wondering: Should I start? By passing on a glass of merlot, am I also saying no to a longer life?

"Abstinence," says David J. Hanson, PhD, "is a health and longevity risk factor." Hanson, a sociology professor who has spent his career researching alcohol and drinking, mentions a Danish study that followed 12,000 people over 20 years. Those who drank moderately and exercised saw their chances of dropping dead from heart disease decrease by 50 percent; exercise-only abstainers like me clocked in at 30 percent. Who would have thought I could optimize my workouts with a beer chaser?

The "healthy happy hour" concept was launched in 1904 when the *Journal of the American Medical Association* ran an article suggesting that alcohol consumption might help prevent heart disease. More than a century later, the research continues to pour in—much of it relevant to my personal health concerns.

I have mild Raynaud's disease, which causes intermittent disruptions in blood circulation to my fingers; a 2007 study in the *American Journal of Medicine* suggests that I may be able to reduce the occurrence of Raynaud's symptoms by downing as little as two glasses of red wine a week. My LDL cholesterol regularly hits the red zone; in 2009, a group of researchers from the University of Connecticut confirmed that not only does resveratrol (a naturally occurring antioxidant in red wine) seem to slow the production of LDL cholesterol, it also helps to increase levels of artery-flushing HDL cholesterol. And yet I persist in washing down my cheddarwurst with Fresca instead of an ice-cold brew.

I was raised in a "dry" church that forbade the use of alcohol. We took grape juice for communion. But this hardly explains my life-long abstinence, as many a devout youth turns to the forbidden fermented fruit at first opportunity. Even my chaste and churchly teen sweetheart was grounded for sneaking beer.

I just never understood drinking. I understood lust and cov-etousness, and even gluttony, but never why you might want to hide behind the high school gymnasium guzzling Boone's Farm until you barfed it all over Tootie Peterson's cheerleading skirt. I wasn't taking a righteous stand—in fact, I partied in the dead-end trailer houses right alongside everyone else—I just had no desire to drink. Watching my varsity football pal Harley hoist a pre-hipster Schlitz in the gravel pit, I felt no temptation to join him. Now I'm over 40, and for the first time I'm feeling peer pressure—not from drunken teenagers but from respected researchers whose medical studies hint that it might be foolish to forgo a little nip.

Still, when you've made it through four decades without a drink, you think twice before imbibing. I hesitate because my family is salted with mildly obsessive-compulsive depressive types (some of us medicated). I also know that when depression and heavy work deadlines intersect, I can go for weeks without surfacing, living on pretty much nothing but Zebra Cakes, coffee, and catnaps.

In my early 30s, I wallowed through a particularly deep trough of depression, holing up for months in my house. Self-pity and a long-gone woman played a part, but my internal chemistry was also awry. I was not suicidal, but I'd reached the point where I didn't particularly care if the Mack truck hit me. One day, quietly desperate for a vacation from my head, I had an "aha" moment: *So this is why people drink.* Then I stepped into my office, and looking at the hovel surrounding me—stacks of unfinished work, unanswered e-mails, unpaid bills, a blinking answering machine, some 20 empty coffee cups (a few of them growing moss), and cellophane wrappers scattered all about—I had another thought: *Hey—maaaybe drinking wouldn't be the best thing for me . . .*

Shortly afterward, I accompanied my friend Al—a connoisseur of small-town bars, cigars, and cold beer—to a local tavern. As I spilled out my troubles and toyed with my water glass, Al listened patiently. I confessed that I was finally tempted to begin drinking.

"Oh, Mikey . . ." said Al, in the tenderest of tones. "There would never be a better time to start!" Raising his beer and displaying it on the palm of his other hand, in the manner of a game show hostess presenting a prize, he said, "Happiness in a can, my friend . . . happiness in a can."

Delightfully bad advice, but I still wasn't ready to cave. Not even for happiness in a can.

But what about *health* in a can?

Professor Leo Sioris, PharmD, gives a lecture at the University of Minnesota called "Wine, Alcohol, and Health." When I see the subtitle of the lecture—"Hey Doc, Should I Start Drinking?"—I give him a call.

"It seems simple," says Dr. Sioris, a clinical toxicologist who keeps a cellar full of red wine. "Do I drink, or not? But in fact that decision depends on your health issues, any medications or supplements you might be taking, and your addiction potential. It really has to be decided between you and your physician."

I am hoping for a more definitive answer, so I perk up when Dr. Sioris adds that in 2002 the New York Academy of Sciences published a series of algorithms intended to take the guesswork out of therapeutic boozing. According to these handy guides, a guy like me (nondrinker over 40 with total cholesterol exceeding 200) can feel free to have one to three drinks a week.

But then at the bottom, in the fine print under "Exclusions," I see this: "nondrinkers with personal history of alcohol problems." Having never had a drink, how do I know if I have a drinking *problem?* I thought of how I pound coffee and sugar until my eyebrows vibrate, and I wondered: *What if it turns out I'm the guy who drinks "just one," loves it, and never stops?*

My sugar habit may indeed be a caution sign. The portion of our brains that feels rewarded by alcohol also determines our reaction to sweets, and according to a Mount Sinai School of Medicine study, my desire for sugar in any form makes me more likely to become an alcoholic than someone who can walk away from the snickerdoodles.

Next I find out that a team at the Ernest Gallo Clinic and Research Center (no problem stocking the lab, I assume) recently discovered a chromosome sequence that was significantly associated with alcoholism. So I contact director Raymond White, PhD, to see if I can submit a tissue sample to establish my odds of ending up a drunk.

"It will be at least a decade before our knowledge is complete enough to give a reasonable indication, and even then there will be uncertainty," says White. "We're even farther back than cardiovascular and cancer researchers in this area of genetic risk assessment."

Even if my genes could hold their liquor, Ezra Amsterdam, MD, wouldn't recommend I start drinking. "There are so many other ways to be heart healthy," says Dr. Amsterdam, associate chief of cardiology at the University of California at Davis medical center. He recently published a review of the research on health and alcohol, and he believes that the advantages of imbibing can easily be overstated—especially if you weren't drinking in the first place.

"There are some possible benefits at a low intake, but there are real downsides," says Dr. Amsterdam. "In the general population, once you go over two drinks a day for men, the risk for practically every disease rises."

• • •

Faced with the conflicting advice of alcohol experts, I finally turn to my wife. She is a moderate drinker and a nutrition fanatic. "Do you think I should start drinking?" I ask, to which she replies, "Not if you handle your drinking anything like you handle your sugar." Recently, she has been forced to hide her baking supplies (specifically, the chocolate-chip bag) in the freezer beneath a fortress of pork chops. I know because that's where I found them one Tuesday at 3 a.m.

But that seals it: I'm going to stay on the wagon. After all these years it'd be a shame to find out I'm that guy who can't hold his booze. And there would be nothing sadder than a man my age woo-hooing in a sports bar.

Besides, the abstemious life has its upside. The first time I was ever called to jury duty it was for a guy fighting a drunk-driving case. Having responded as an EMT to alcohol-related crashes for years, and having worked at least one accident scene with the arresting deputy, I figured I'd be bounced right away. But I made it into the final group and was seated. Just as the judge swiveled his chair to begin the trial, he paused, and swiveled back to look at us in the jury box. "Just out of curiosity," he said, "is there anyone here who doesn't drink?"

I raised my hand. I was the only one.

"Do you believe if someone drinks alcohol they are a bad person?" asked the judge.

"If I did," I replied, "I wouldn't have any friends."

That got a pretty good laugh. But then, with the comic timing of a veteran standup, the judge replied, "Not in this county you wouldn't!"

That got an even bigger laugh.

And then he bounced me.

2010

LIKE MOTHER, LIKE SON

Should you ever find me trapped within the crushed chassis of a 1974 AMC Gremlin, please dial 911. Then call my mom. If the fire department will kindly lend her the Jaws of Life, Mom will rip the doors from the car. I have seen her do this before.

You wouldn't predict behavior of this sort just by looking at my mother. She is a petite and devout woman, given to pinning her hair up and wearing modest dresses. But when she heard that my brother John and I were taking a class to become emergency medical technicians, she said, "I've always wanted to do something with my boys," and then enrolled with us. Thus we found ourselves slack-jawed one morning down at the vocational college watching Mom, clad in a hard hat and goggles, hydraulic ram braced against one thigh, shredding that Gremlin like Church Lady meets American Hot Rod.

You wanna call me a mama's boy?

I'm fine with that.

I'd like to say I am all man, but 50 percent of me, genetically speaking, is 100 percent Mom. I am reminded of this every morning when I look in the mirror and see her unibrow reclining above my eyes like a caterpillar on a deck chair. (Mom bisected hers with electrolysis years ago.) I also inherited her small hands and feet (I know what you're thinking, and it isn't nice), as well as an unfortunate tendency to perspire aggressively in stressful social situations. ("Focal hyperhidrosis"—I had it checked.)

There's more. We share a pair of conditions (Raynaud's disease, in which arterial spasms cause our fingers to go clammy, and Gilbert syndrome, a benign liver disorder). Our cholesterol levels run high, we are prone to fits of anxiety and depression, we're constantly sidetracked by attention-deficit tangents, and we both have developed addictions to caffeine. Finally, Mom has a habit of flicking her hands against her legs when she is discomfited. Both John and I have inherited versions of this tic, effectively killing our chances of achieving success in the world of high-stakes poker. My father, a man possessed of two natural eyebrows and a Buddha-like calm, has none of these afflictions.

Shared DNA is a given, but what about the more intangible aspects of our personalities? Is it possible for a boy to be nurtured into manhood?

Most men spend their childhoods trying to emulate their father in all things, unless Dad is absent or an utter thug. One of my enduring memories is of standing in the bathroom, tilting my head back to watch my father as he shaved. It is a moment millions of young boys experience. When I grow up, we think, I'm going to be just like him. Much rarer is the boy who looks at Mom and thinks, When I grow up, I'm going to be just like her.

But what do we miss by leaving Mom out of the equation? She may not teach you how to run a razor (although when I shaved my legs for a bike race, Mom did warn me against certain depilatories), but if you watch her closely, you'll learn that not only does it take more than muscles and a five o'clock shadow to make a real man, but sometimes it takes a real woman. For the first 39 years of my life, until I got married, that woman was my mother.

Having just described my mom as a palsied bundle of neuroses, allow me to expand the picture. Over the years she has taken responsibility for the care and feeding of legions of children at our farm—some conceived, some adopted, some fostered, and some delivered by the county for the weekend or for a lifetime. She is demure and slight of build, but in her work as an EMT I have watched three firefighters rush to her with an unconscious baby and then enclose her in a semicircle of hulking apprehension while she calmly breathed the baby back to life. (Paradoxically, our anxious tendencies evaporate in the face of blood and carnage, while Dad the Buddha goes queasy.) I have also seen her up to her elbow in the rear end of a sheep and giving rescue breaths to a newborn Holstein calf. (Not simultaneously, mind you.)

Many of the children my parents took in were severely ill or disabled. Our house often had the look of a pediatrics ward. Green oxygen bottles lined the porch. A lazy Susan on the counter was covered with medication bottles, and there was digitalis in the refrigerator. A registered nurse by training, Mom left a hospital career to care for these children at home full-time. She was forever coming from and going to doctor appointments and blood draws. I accompanied her on many of these trips while Dad stayed back to milk the cows and care for the rest of the crew. Once when my sister Rya took a precipitous turn for the worse, I held her as Mom drove 40 miles through a blizzard to an emergency room. When I chose to pursue a degree in nursing, I wasn't thinking of gender roles—I was thinking of my mother's example. On my first day of nursing school, I found a line of graffiti in the men's locker room—*male nurses are homos.* Rather than take offense, I remember thinking that (a) I could kick the crap out of the knucklehead who wrote that, and (b) my mother, who day after day cared for her ill babies, showed me that strength is not always muscular and bravery is not always brash.

Lest things get too gauzy, I also had more than one opportunity to watch her shuck her natural reticence and go toe-to-toe with physicians who made the mistake of condescending to her in matters of her children's health. As a result, when a notoriously nasty doctor began yelling at me during my first year as a nurse, I thought of my mother, stomped my inner wimp, looked him in the eye, and told him that when he was ready to converse in a collegial manner he could find me in room 912, caring for my patient. I won that round, thanks to Mom.

◆ ◆ ◆

My mother and I are not alike in all things. She is a devout Christian woman whose single most powerful epithet is "Oh, fiddlesticks!" I am a bumbling agnostic who tries not to swear in public but will peel the paint in private. In all my life I have never heard Mom indulge in even the most innocent double entendre or off-color comment. (The fact that she says something is "bollixed" doesn't count, as I can assure you she is oblivious to the fact that it is derivative of the mild English expletive "bollocks," and if she reads this she will be mortified.)

When she discovered that a song on one of our children's albums contained an objectionable rhyme, she cut a groove in the song with a pin. The phonograph needle skidded right past the track with a scratchy rumble. If you were to confront my mother and accuse her of censorship, she would reply, "Exactly."

Once in the early stages of losing my religion, I attended a church event wearing long, spiked hair and dressed like a cross between a U2 roadie and Don Johnson's personal valet. I was sitting by Mom when she quietly wondered what the other worshipers must think of my attire. "I don't care what these people think!" I snapped, and she turned her head quickly, but I had seen the immediate flash of tears and I was sick with my cruelty.

I have also failed to inherit my mother's sense of economy. For 40 years she has raised a constantly fluctuating passel of tots, drawing on her wits, 25-pound bags of oatmeal, and a fistful of coupons the size of a bad Uno hand. To say she was thrifty is to understate: Whenever one of us spilled our juice, Mom would grab a spoon and scrape madly at the spreading slick, ladling the juice back into the glass so it could be drunk. The same thing happened if someone spilled milk. Sometimes when I wonder how my parents managed financially, I think of Mom going after our Kool-Aid like an environmentalist trailing the Exxon *Valdez*.

I do not scoop up orange juice, but I have compensated by marrying a thrifty woman. While other husbands go ballistic over nasty surprises on the credit card, I am reduced to waving the Visa bill and barking, "$7.95 at Goodwill?!? That's the second time this year!" Like most well-worn tropes, the idea that men marry a dead ringer for dear old Mom is probably only half accurate at best, but when I go to the kitchen sink and find plastic bread bags air-drying on the faucet handles (the twist ties stored neatly in the drawer), I will admit to the ol' deja vu.

When it comes to my parents, I like to say anything decent in me is because of them; everything else is simply not their fault. I am not a rescue hotshot, but I do okay at accident scenes, thanks to Mom's genes (the innate ability to keep my lunch down) and her example (we subvert our nervous-Nellie tendencies long enough to get the job done). Were Dad my only influence, I would not be considered bold and brave—I would respond to bloody emergencies by taking a nap. Maybe your mother didn't attack cars with a giant can opener, but chances are if you spend a little time looking for Mom in the mirror, you'll discover that without her, you would be half the man you are today.

2009

WORKING

Viewed from a distance of 25 yards, my brother Jed and I are obviously sprung from the same womb. Same balding round crania, same nose, same gapped teeth, same general frame. Zoom into our hands, however, and singular distinctions emerge. At base, they are the same size. Similar smallish bone structure. But Jed's fingers are thickened to half again the circumference of mine. The heels of his hands (what the anatomy books call the thenar and hypothenar eminences) are meatier (more eminent) than mine. His palms are scored and rough.

Mine? Well, let's just say they look more suited to cradling kittens than cranking a cant hook.

In the course of general social exchange, the questions "What do you do?" or "What are you?" are nearly always answered in terms of work:

"I farm."

"I paint."

"I am a carpenter."

"I am a social worker."

Answers from another angle ("I breathe deeply," "I am a satisfied man") will be received with skepticism and discomfort.

Where I come from, it is always tricky when a person with soft hands delivers a discourse on hard work. When I say "where I come from," I'm talking not so much about the map as the society. Never mind that decades have passed since I last worked on a sawmill, or branded a calf, or milked a cow—those physical labors remain the standard against which I weigh all work, even as I gratefully support myself by rearranging electrons by fingertip.

I have just returned from a visit to the Wyoming ranch where I worked for five summers from the age of sixteen. It was good to visit and catch up, and resurrect old memories, but I felt more comfortable helping dig postholes than I did sitting in the visitor's chair. When I visit a farm, nothing relieves me more than to be asked to pitch in. To throw some hay bales or move some sod, or maybe rake hay. This desire is rooted in my memories of city people who would show up at our farm in light clothing and look at a pitchfork as if it was radioactive. Their apparent lack of embarrassment at being seen to just sit around made me jumpy and self-conscious on their behalf.

And that's a problem, too.

My problem.

We value work inconsistently, choosing to ignore—or overlook, or leave unremarked—the fact that vast swaths of the nation's earning power are underpinned by unpaid and underpaid work. We hail the grand captain of industry while overlooking the person who empties his paper shredder, we nod reverently at the successful farmer down at the café while back home his wife is tending fires fueling the entire operation.

When I shake hands with someone and feel the thick scuff of calluses, I think of the people who raised me and adopt a reflexive humility and admiration. But even this can swerve quickly into self-serving condescension, as if by applying the "noble" tag to physical labor—perhaps, say, by writing a brief essay on the subject—we excuse ourselves to let anyone but us do it.

Where I come from, you admire hard physical labor. I like that I am imbued with that. It is essentially grounding. But there is also the danger of developing a reverse snobbery against anyone with soft hands. There is the tendency to conflate admiration for hard physical labor with disdain for intellectual and artistic pursuits.

To sneer at book-learnin', no matter that some PhD genius designed the turbo on your pickup truck. It is out of this consciousness that I tend to refer to myself not as a writer or an author but as a self-employed typist, which is fine and self-deprecating to a point, but when extrapolated without limits undermines those who work hard with their hearts and minds—and I'm not just talking about your received artists: I mean to include people who show up and do the figurative heavy lifting required to spackle the gaps between labor and capital, up to and including—dare I say it—dedicated and much-maligned government workers.

And city people.

No matter how I struggle over the form and content of the essay at hand, I will be hard-pressed to elicit an empathetic nod from my brother the logger—his skull X-rays still featuring the hairline split laid there by the butt end of a widowmaker, his throat scarred by the sapling that ran him through like a spear in a freak logging accident (as if there weren't enough standard logging accidents), and of course the clicks, lumps, and strains bound to infiltrate any body employed for decades in the most elemental sort of hard work. And yet it is interesting how the ultimate manifestation of the respective physical damage work has exacted from the two of us—his a kinetic toll of fractures, falls, lacerations, and general knockabout; mine the creaks, kinks, and impingements accumulated from decades of slumping in place—is that we both walk like aging loggers.

Both of us shaped by our work.

The soft hands. It always comes back to that. Sometimes if I spend a few days straight running a shovel, or splitting wood, or helping the neighbor hay, at night I will feel my hands swelling with the work. And when the blisters shift to callus, it feels good. When I sit down to type with those hands, I don't pretend to be a laborer, but I can hope that whatever words I generate will be inflected by the experience.

And maybe that's it: perhaps the best reason to study the concept of "work" is to expand our understanding of its many manifestations and permutations. In my case, to pry the term away from the pitchfork handle. To focus less on the position and the paycheck and more on the drive and the need.

To understand why someone works at what they do for the reasons they do is to develop empathy.

And what more noble work can there be than the manufacture of empathy?

2014

A PHILOSOPHER FOR THE REST OF US

This piece began as a paragraph in my book Visiting Tom. *Then it grew into my book* Montaigne in Barn Boots. *In between it took this form in* Men's Health Magazine.

Recently while feeding my pigs, I was moved to consider Michel de Montaigne's essay "That to Study Philosophy Is to Learn to Die." As a barn-booted dude who counts a second-place finish in the sixth grade spelling bee as an intellectual pinnacle, I wouldn't expect to have a lot in common with a 16th-century French philosopher who spoke Latin as a first language, went to college at the age of 6, and studied law when he was 14. He also held several high-level government positions, hung out (just once, but still . . .) with the pope, and retired to his country estate at the age of 38 to write essays. (In fact, Montaigne is credited with inventing the essay.)

As you might expect, Montaigne tussled in his scrivenings with humankind's universal biggies—freedom, power, religion, the nature of existence—and he regularly backed his observations with quotes from the likes of Homer, Cicero, and Lucretius. But he also left us with his thoughts on such topics as hairstyles, farting, impotence, aromatherapy, and politics.

Also, killer pigs. That day in my hog pen, the porkers were so hungry and impatient for their mash that they began shoulder-checking me in the shins and nibbling at my kneecaps, reminding me of the long list of unfortunate people Montaigne had rattled off in the aforementioned essay. These folks had died under unusual circumstances: choking on a grape seed, scratched by a comb, hit by a falling turtle, and—pertinent to my situation—"by jostle of a hog." One suspects it wasn't so much the "jostle" as what happened after the jostle that did him in, but still, I felt the chill snout of death. To strengthen my spirits as I forged onward to the slop trough, I focused on the fact that in the selfsame essay, Montaigne cited no fewer than six men who—in the Department of Something to Shoot For—perished "betwixt the very thighs of women."

And this is what I like about Montaigne: He charges us to consider the power of philosophy as it pertains to preparing ourselves to confront our mortality—and then he reminds us that mortality itself may arrive in the form of angry bacon. He also saw the mullet coming from 400 years away.

Drawing from a 1600s translation of his renowned essays, I hereby present vintage advice on modern topics, otherwise known as "Montaigne on . . ."

FASHION

Long before Kardashians roamed the land, Montaigne fretted that style was outstripping substance ("I hate our people, who can worse endure an ill-contrived robe than an ill-contrived mind"), and he wrote worriedly of the "delicate and affected" men who "caused their hair to be pinched off." Ultimately he opted for a simple look. "I desire therein to be viewed as I appear in mine own genuine, simple, and ordinary manner, without study and artifice . . . I seldom wear other than black or white." In other words, he really did care about style, with one simple rule: If it makes you feel silly, don't wear it.

HAIRSTYLES

Perhaps because he was a bit of a cue ball ("my old bald grizzled likeness"), Montaigne was especially grumpy about coiffure.

In "Of Ancient Customs," he describes people who "wore their hair long before and the hinder part of the head shaved, a fashion that begins to revive in this vicious and effeminate age." As a guy who was once all business in the front and party in the back, I have to wonder: Which came first—the mullet or the reverse mullet? Anticipating the 1980s (or perhaps even Bieber bangs), Montaigne went on to warn us that "there will often be a necessity that the despised forms must again come in vogue." Thus we await the return of the man-perm.

MARRIAGE

When his friends criticized him for taking too many road trips and leaving his wife behind, Montaigne insisted that he was strengthening his marriage, since "being continually together is not so pleasing as to part for a time and meet again." Of course, he also wrote, "Every strange woman appears charming," speaking for generations of horndogs to come, including professional baseball players and rock stars.

POLITICS

After 17 years in politics and law, Montaigne wrote that he would far rather face "an enemy in arms, than an enemy in a gown." Nominated for and elected mayor of Bordeaux while he was away on vacation, Montaigne taught us the most important political lesson of all: Never miss a meeting, or you will find yourself in charge of the office Christmas party.

SEX

Although he claimed to be a sensitive lover ("The pleasure I give tickles my imagination more sweetly than that which I feel"), Montaigne believed that a man shouldn't try anything too fancy with his wife, avoiding "immodest and debauched tricks and postures . . . lest . . . the extreme pleasure make her exceed the bounds of reason." Yes. Well. Now I can tell my wife I'm not underperforming; I'm protecting her sanity. Of course, if you really want to learn how to please a woman, skip the philosophy and talk to her.

SNOT

Yes, Montaigne even waxed philosophical about boogers and their proper disposal. "A French gentleman was always wont to blow his nose with his fingers, and he justifying himself for so doing . . . asked me, what privilege this filthy excrement had, that we must carry about us a fine handkerchief to receive it . . . and carry it all day about in our pockets. . . . I found that what he said was not altogether without reason." Handkerchiefs make lovely do-rags and fine pocket squares; for everything else, use a tissue.

ERECTILE DYSFUNCTION

Montaigne missed the Golden Age of ED by 400 years, but he knew men were equipped with a tool of variable reliability, calling it "so unseasonably disobedient, when we stand most in need of it." He recommended that a man who makes "an ill beginning" and is "baffled at the first assault" should "leisurely and by degrees make several little trials and light offers" until the equipment cooperates. He also cured an impotent but gullible friend by convincing him to conduct a series of silly rituals prior to climbing into bed. Apparently, Montaigne already understood the brain as a sex organ.

PREMATURE EJACULATION

"In the critical moment," Montaigne wrote, ". . . think of something else." Decent tip, although you wish he'd specified what to think about, since baseball hadn't been invented yet. Jousting, perhaps, but the imagery is metaphorically problematic.

WORK

In the context of the times, Montaigne was respected as a man who took his duties as a landowner and a politician seriously, and he worked hard to dispatch them fairly. But then, at the age of 38 (supported, it must be said, by a major cash stash), he chucked it all to do whatever he wanted and wound up becoming one of the most famous writers of all time.

MAN CAVES

Prior to the availability of neon beer signs on eBay, Montaigne put together a sweet book-lined hangout in a hard-to-reach castle tower, complete with battle murals and a bed so he could crash anytime he wanted. He loved to be alone ("to disengage and disobligate myself") and even claimed it a relief when a friend mistreated him, as this meant he didn't have to hang out with the guy anymore. So you're not hiding out in the garage, you're being philosophical.

MONEY

When Montaigne came into money, he quickly found himself turning into an anxious hoarder: "The more I loaded myself with money, the more also was I loaded with fear [of losing it]." Then, after splurging on a very expensive trip, he found himself "fallen into a third way of living" in which he spent freely if not wildly, and found himself happier. Keep an eye on your 401(k), Montaigne would say, but go ahead and buy the sports car.

FARTING

Montaigne had the usual frat-boy fascination with flatulence. He noted that St. Augustine spoke of "having seen a man who could command his rear to discharge as often together as he pleased." But he also believed stifled toots were deadly ("how often a man's belly, by the denial of one single puff, brings him to the very door of an exceeding painful death") and thus admired the Emperor Claudius, who "gave liberty to let fly in all places." Frankly, Montaigne's fears seem overblown, so to speak, and I'd hate to have been trapped in a carriage with him.

PORN

When young boys drew naughty pictures on the castle walls, Montaigne was troubled not by the vandalism or sex as much as the "prodigious dimension" of the anatomy, as they "give the ladies a cruel contempt of our natural furniture." The take-home for 2012: If you want to watch porn with a woman, view it on a laptop, not a 52-inch LCD TV.

FOOD

In *How to Live,* biographer Sarah Bakewell notes that when Montaigne traveled, he made a point of eating native food prepared in the native manner. He thought it a vice "not to make good cheer with what another is enjoying," and that we should "be curious in what a man eats." So eat local and don't be picky and, like Montaigne, you too can live to be, er, 59.

PROJECT "YOU"

I first discovered Montaigne while reading . . . um . . . well, I can't remember what I was reading. This happens to me a lot, and would bother me, but then as Montaigne himself wrote, "If I am a man of some reading, I am a man of no retention." And right there is probably why I like Montaigne most of all: By ruthlessly excavating every corner of his life (dude would have run a top-notch Tumblr) and holding it up for examination, by working hard to better himself even if he doesn't improve, Montaigne reminds us that even though we are works in progress, the work of self-improvement is more important than the progress.

2012

P.S. Later while going through some old notes I recalled that I discovered Montaigne because of a kidney stone. That's another story, in another book. I also learned that 16th-century "college" didn't mean what I thought it did (more like grade school), but he was still an overachiever.

FAITH AND MUSIC

GREG BROWN: HALLELUJAH ANYWAY

When as a young child you are called by the Lord to rise from
your metal folding chair in the basement of the Moose Hall and
commit your life to Christ upon the commencement of the final
chorus of "Close Thy Heart No More," you remain forever sus-
ceptible to the lexicon of faith.

All subsequent straying will not alter this fact.

You are hooked on the *thee* and *thou,* and always will be. You
will toddle along into a life of scuffing and sinning and just keep
on a-wandering, and one day you will hear someone railing on
those scary fundamentalist Christians and you will pick up your
bumbling agnostical head from its existential dreamland, and you
will say, Hey those are my people you're talking about.

And you will look back down the path you have trodden, and
you will not be able to feature the circumstances under which you
would return to faith and fold, but likewise you cannot imagine
where you would stand lacking the reckoning points set by both.

Having wrassled this contradiction every day since the Moose
Hall, you will remain peeved with those who think you left the
flock because you are a silly little sheep, but you will be grateful
for the foundation the church provided, even as you stack your
bricks in the sand.

There is a certain vocabulary you learn only through attrition
and heartache, and Greg Brown speaks it. His music is suffused

with what singer Dar Williams calls "the mercy of the fallen." Wisdom can arise from contradiction—*Covenant,* one of Brown's loveliest albums, is a testament to enduring love written by a man heading into his third marriage. The fallible prophets of my youth cured me of confusing the singer with the song long ago. For all I know Greg Brown is a difficult angel or a randy scoundrel, but that music of his is dead true, and I am eager to hear him speak.

We meet on a park bench, in the middle of what passes for a park, in what passes for Iowa City, although it is hardly the Iowa City of Greg Brown's skinny days. Later, while transcribing the interview, I will hear the calls of children clambering on the super-safe playground toys, and even on the poor-quality tape you can tell the voices are bouncing off the glass canyon formed by the big flat Sheraton and the avant Hotel Vetro, which is as swank a place as you'd expect given the stainless steel and the prefix positioning of the word "hotel." "High rises could change the face of Iowa City," it said across the front page of the *Iowa City Press-Citizen* this morning. Cornfields, shmornfields.

It's a big man on the bench beside me, big but not imposing. Showing a little age, the beard grizzled, the eyebrows frayed some. Wearing a porkpie hat, straw. A pinstriped navy suit coat, hand stitched around the collar and open to a tank-style undershirt. Crocs with socks. Sunglasses. He was reading the newspaper when I approached. It is folded now, stuffed inside his backpack. He draws at coffee from a cardboard cup, and now and then lights a cigarette.

For the first five minutes of our conversation, I am distracted by intermittent vibrations passing through the slats of the bench back. It feels as if we are above a subway, or perhaps the Hotel Vetro (VAY-tro, thanks very much) is settling on its fresh foundations. And then I realize the tremors occur whenever Greg Brown speaks. Boy, now that would be something. To have a voice that could rattle the slats in a park bench.

There are over 25 albums now, and enough reviews and pro-files to stock a small reference library, to say nothing of catch-all Web pages and discussion threads and anecdotes and rumors and citations, and nearly always there is reference to that voice.

It has been cast in terms of bullfrogs, gathering storms, and Howlin' Wolf. Brown's barrel-deep and lazy-lipped delivery on the first two tracks of *The Evening Call* (his latest album with Red House Records) spawned online chatter including the possibility that Brown recorded with a cold, or had undergone dental work. Other listeners chalked up the changes to studio effects. One contributor offered a syllable-by-syllable breakdown (including diagrams) of how Brown was creating the particular sound using vibrato, falsetto, slurs, and pitch.

These attentions speak to the reaction his instrument com-pels. It owes something to technique, sure enough, but above all Brown turns himself over, lets the voice find its character and speak as it will. It isn't all about getting down low. In a line from the title track, his voice descends through the line "how low the sun," then rises from the subterranean registers to moan in the key of beseechment.

At its classic best, Brown's baritone swells like a foghorn from a socked-in shore, a rumble implying that the big trouble rarely comes crashing like a comet from the sky, but rather waits with malevolent patience beneath the surface. Waves come and go, but beware the undertow. And even those times when he gets to rocking back on his chair and, well, *bleating,* you are heartened by a man willing to abandon himself to whatever spirit that might be.

Beyond volume and tone, Brown's vocal power is further amped by the manner in which he employs it in the parsing of lyrics. "Eugene" is a warm, rambling spoken-word piece. No mel-ody, as such, but each line rewards close listening. Working a lazy-day groove, Brown infuses the recitation with all sorts of unexpected, understated richness: letting a little extra air slide across his vocal cords so the sound goes chalky, or the way he blows a "b" or lisps an "s," the way he lets the tail end of the word "horizon" slip up from his throat and slide out his nose. The rhythmic changeup he throws when he hits the line "and a good sharp knife"—ba-da-BUMP-bump-bump—and then the final line, in which he uses the words as a form of percussion, making each syllable serve the rhythm. You are not surprised to hear him name-check poets.

"I had those Caedmon recordings when I was a boy," says Brown. "I had e.e. cummings and Dylan Thomas records, and I listened to those like I listened to my Rolling Stones records." He leans forward and declaims grandly, "'Now as I was young and easy under the apple boughs . . .' Yeah, Dylan Thomas. A real singer.

"Poets I like, people like Gary Snyder or Ferlinghetti, Pablo Neruda, William Butler Yeats, William Carlos Williams . . . if you get a chance to hear these people read, they're singing. I love that old style of singing a poem, which went up strongly through people like Yeats and Pound."

He leans forward again, chanting Yeats: "'I will arise and go now, and go to Innisfree, and a small cabin build there, of clay and wattles made . . .'" Brown is grinning, delighted. "Y'know, he's singin' the thing! That makes my little hairs go up. Pablo Neruda, whether you speak Spanish or not, it'll make you weep to hear him sing his poems. These academic poets now, I've gone to several readings, and I get the giggles sometimes, because the verse is so flat, and they read it in this flat, uncomfortable way. A little stilted. Where's the music, man?"

I was raised a fundamentalist Christian boy in a sect so ascetically badass, we were taking the Christ out of Christmas long before the term "secular humanist" even existed. We had no name, we did not believe in church buildings or preachers in vestments, and we did not decorate trees.

We gathered in regular houses and sat in straight-back chairs, constructed our own homilies and offered our own prayers. We practiced full-immersion baptism, televisions and radios were forbidden, and our sacraments were bread and grape juice, because alcohol was the devil's gargle.

We sang unadorned hymns, a cappella. You'd hear the men grinding away at the harmonies down below and the younger women rounding out the middle range. And high above it all (I am thinking especially of the times we held meetings in a barn, and the sound had room to rise) the melody, carried by old women in plain dresses singing in guileless falsetto. They took it right to the rafters.

You ease away. Years pass. You read *Being and Nothingness.* Then one day several years after its release, you get a copy of Iris DeMent's *Infamous Angel.* And when Flora Mae DeMent's voice comes soaring out those speakers, you are right back in the barn, ready to rise and profess again: *Lord, plant my feet on higher ground.*

And yet you crave the wisdom of sinners.

Greg Brown, too, was raised up in the church. He can speak the King James, give you a little *shalt* and *wilt.* His beloved grandmother was a Southern Baptist. His father was a preacher, Pentecostal. "My dad was very unusual in that he was not tryin' to scare anybody into heaven," says Brown. "He always approached the Bible as beautiful stories we could learn a lot from. At the end of his life he had gone from Southern Baptist to open Bible, to Methodist, to Baha'i. And the Baha'i religion is open arms to everybody. That was his path, and I grew up under his guidance. But I also saw a lot of these like the guy I spoof in 'Inabell,' a lot of these Elmer Gantry type of people."

By the age of 20, Greg left church life behind. For good, he thought. Did not intend to return, he says. But during last night's show at the Englert Theatre—just a block from this bench—he was tuning his guitar when he mentioned that he has joined a church in Kansas City. A church where the preacher sometimes prays that the bombs falling in Iraq might rather take the form of buses and groceries. This is a prayer requiring great faith.

Having once been born again, I have little interest in the testimony of someone freshly so. One still blinded by the light. But the testimony of someone who has been born again, unborn, then reborn . . .

Brown also said from the stage that he didn't believe in heaven per se. And then he hung his suit jacket over a chair and proceeded to deliver an arm-waving spoken-word interpretation of "Inabell Sale" in the character of an exasperated psychobilly Bible-thumper, and he flat-out inhabited the role, skipping and raving and clapping his hands to his head, and by the time he wrapped it up, you figured had he not strayed into a life of playing music for us transgressors, that Reverend Brown's boy, he coulda brought some folks to Jesus.

And then, right on cue, a breaker blew, and all the lights went out.

"It was just a joke, Lord," said Brown from the dark.

The veracity of Brown's music has always been bolstered by a sense of literacy. You will find it in *The Evening Call* when he pins human nature in "Whippoorwill" ("If you ever leave/And I imagine you will"), makes the smart rhyme in "Pound It on Down" ("Cut the rope/Kick the boat"), or nails the details (the gunpowder tea in "Eugene," the tube top in "Kokomo"). When choosing his words, Brown rarely exercises the standard options. You get the sense he hones those lines, again and again.

Not so, he says. Take, for instance, that gunpowder tea. "I just wrote that song out as fast as I could write," he says. "I'd had this image in my mind for a while of a trip and going to the places where, when I'm out touring, I don't have time to explore as much as I'd like to. My mind was just drifting along with that idea, and one day I just sat down with my notebook, and I didn't think of it as something I would do music with, it was just kind of a free-flow deal. And when I finished it, I thought, Hmmm, I wonder what this would be like if you put some music behind it.

"I'm not much of a detail editor. I'm a groove singer and player and writer. Once I can find the groove, I feel like I'm just ridin' in my little boat. Sometimes, with certain songs I've written over the years, like 'My New Book,' or 'Milk of the Moon,' or 'Rexroth's Daughter,' they've gone through many, many versions. Probably dozens and dozens of discarded verses. But if I do feel like I'm gettin' the groove a little bit, I'll stick with something. I'll keep cuttin' and hackin' and tryin'."

And then he'll revise on the fly. Just when you're taken with that gunpowder tea, he drops it. Last night, for instance. It wasn't there. "That was the first time I played 'Eugene' live," says Brown. "I ended up putting a lot of different things in there that weren't in the way I recorded it. And that's probably the way that song will be. It can change depending on the night. New details will come in, other things will drift away. With me, it's just the way I'm trying to catch that groove, and once I do that, then I'm free, really, and whatever's gonna come up that particular night has got an open door."

Brown's ability to conjure vérité sometimes leads his fans to speculation and fact-checking. To separate the real from the made-up. "That whole thing, that whole issue, y'know, I . . ." He trails off for a minute, then gets rolling again. "I don't think it matters in terms of where a song starts, if it's actual details, actual people I know or not. That's not really the point with songs. If they're not bigger than that, then . . ."

He thinks a bit. "If there's not room in songs for other people, then they ain't gonna listen to 'em. It's just that simple. There are certain people who've thought they were in a song. I generally don't try to dissuade anyone if they wanna think that. But it's not what I'm up to. Things I wanna say in a letter to somebody, I say in a letter."

Last night's show at the Englert was a homecoming of sorts. Brown was long a part of the Iowa City scene, playing at the Mill and living outside of town in the eponymous little red house of Red House Records, the mainstay purveyor of Brown's work. (Brown's tender eulogy for longtime friend and label president Bob Feldman, who died in January, is on the inside flap of *The Evening Call*.) Brown moved out of Iowa City a few years ago, and it's no secret that he doesn't think Iowa City is aging well.

"In some ways it's almost like coming back to a different town," he says. "I mean this stuff"—he waves at the carpeted playground before him and the Hotel Vetro behind him—"all this stuff was not here. The town has gotten kind of mallish. I remember this town when it had a lot more architecturally. And there were a lot more characters. It just kinda looks like a lot of other places now. And the police force had gotten overly aggressive, I thought. You could hardly walk down the street without getting a ticket for something or other. The town had taken a right turn, I'd say, politically and pro-development, et cetera, et cetera. When I left, I was ready to go."

When Brown played the song "Your Town Now" last night, an insider's chuckle rippled around the room. But Brown cautions against a literal autobiographical take. "That had been my plan for a while—when my youngest graduated, I was going to move down to my grandparents' farm and build a house, and I did all that.

"My attachment to my friends and my family members who live here, those attachments are undying, and they're not really even dependent upon a place so much. I actually wrote that song several years before I left and wasn't thinking so much of the town not being here as I was kind of handing the baton to the next generation. I really wrote the song mostly for a guy named Dave Zollo [the Iowa City musician who started Trailer Records] and other young musicians. It was like, well, it's kinda up to you now."

These days Brown splits his days between time on the road, a farmhouse in the Iowa countryside, and a home in Kansas City with his wife (singer Iris DeMent) and their young daughter. "I basically think your sense of place has to be inside you," he says. "On the other hand, Hacklebarney, which is my grandparents' old farm where I live part of the time now, that kind of sense of place . . . that little farm goes back in my family to statehood and it's true, I feel things there I just don't feel anywhere else. I have connections there that run very deep."

If the accumulated works of Greg Brown are to be hung on the pintle of the fact that he is Iowegian by birth and Midwestern by raising, it should be said this is but the bolt on which the rudder pivots. He is an omnivorous American hybrid. You can see it in his dress, hear it in his lyrics, and detect it in his vocalizations: plenty of seed corn cap and loam, but also the Greenwich Village bohemian, the San Francisco beat. The cantankerous rustic and the hopeful hippie. The calloused hand, the polished mind. If a Greg Brown song was just some guy, he'd be rocked back in a chair on a porch at dusk, his head would be full with the scent of tilled soil, and he would have some old book open over one knee.

"I've just been reading Henry Miller's *Air-Conditioned Nightmare,* which is a brilliant book. It was written in the 1940s, but it could have been written yesterday. I go back and read Henry Miller every few years. I'm hoping someday I'm going to feel enough inward strength to go back and read *Jude the Obscure* again. It's the darkest book you can imagine. After Thomas Hardy wrote that, there was such an outcry in England, he never wrote another novel. He turned to poetry—which I'm grateful for, because he's a great poet. I like reading Thomas Hardy in the fall. His books always make me feel like autumn somehow.

"I go back and read the poems of Villon translated by Galway Kinnell. I've tried to set some of those to music. Vallejo, his poems are like they're written out of rock and metal and electricity. Lately, I've been reading Bukowski again. I mean, he's only got this one little story: He got drunk, he went to the track, he listened to classical music, and then he woke up the next day and did it all again. But I love the way he tells it. Marina Tsvetaeva, she was a poet in the teens, '20s, '30s, a great, great poet. And Larry Brown was a writer I liked very much. I was just sick when he died.

"The poets and writers I've come across in my life, I feel a companionship with these people, just as I do with a lot of musicians and songwriters. I've never made much of a differentiation out of, say, the songs of a Walt Whitman or a Pablo Neruda and the songs of a Bob Dylan or a Hank Williams."

It wasn't on the set list last night, but in the song "Billy from the Hills," there is a line about pitching camp at a fork in the river where knowledge meets remorse. If that makes you gulp and check your rearview mirror, welcome to being a grown-up. Greg Brown sings of things earned as much as learned, and often the hard way.

There is this misperception among the faithful that when you go astray you lose your heart. But you can reject the dogma and still retain a deep reverence for the price of transgression. Whether your roller coaster is headed down or up, Greg Brown's music says I can't believe I did that, or even more to the point, I can't believe I did that *again,* and look at the state of things, but—as I once heard him sing at the end of the despairing "Homeland"—"Hallelujah . . . hallelujah . . . hallelujah anyway."

Is there a more beautiful word than hallelujah? Just the saying of it thrills the residual believer in me. We crave the incantations. But the part of me that can never go back loves that final "anyway."

If I have the math right, Flora Mae DeMent would be Greg Brown's third mother-in-law. When I tell him how her singing transported me, he smiles. "I think in those hymns there is a great sense of longing. A very honest, open longing. Because here we are, we don't know what's goin' on, there's all these stories—when we die, we're goin' here, we're goin' there . . . we don't know. And those songs have a beautiful ache to them. When Iris sings, you hear all that. It just opens people's hearts up, whatever their religious views may be. That deep longing in there, that speaks to the human soul, and that's a beautiful thing.

"I never thought in my life I would go to church again. I think it was Mary McCarthy said, 'Religion's only good for good people.' And that's true, I think. My grandmother Ella Mae was a Southern Baptist in the Ozarks, and she was a great and kind person. She believed in those Bible stories and they were a big part of her life. She was a real good person.

"At any rate, the organized church, I was pretty much done with it by the time I was 20. In Kansas City, Iris had started going to a church called St. Mark's. The preacher there is a white guy, Sam Mann, who came to Kansas City 35 years ago on a motor-cycle as a Methodist preacher. He was a young buck, started preachin' against the Vietnam War, got kicked out by the Meth-odists. Scrambled around, there was a black church, St. Mark's, their preacher had died or left, and Sam went there as a substi-tute. They kept tryin' to find a preacher there and couldn't find anybody. And finally, they liked Sam so much they said, why don't you be our preacher?

"So Sam has been the preacher at this church for 35 years now. An amazing fellow, he preaches out of the Bible, but he doesn't care at all about the whole story of when Jesus went up into heaven and all that. He approaches it as this world. Right now. That's where heaven, and hell, and salvation, and all the rest of it is. It's a beautiful thing for me to be back in a church where there's something going on. But it's based on this life. And this earth.

"That fits in with my beliefs, which is that it's all right here right now. It's not about some afterlife. When Thoreau was on his deathbed, they asked him about dying, he said, 'One world at a time.' They asked him, have you made your peace with God, he said, 'We've never quarreled.'

"And I feel pretty much that way. I don't try to define God, or the Great Being, or anything like that, but I do feel that we're in a very big and very beautiful mystery here. And acceptance of that, and some sort of bow, I think in this life is very important. I don't care if you're bowin' to an oak tree, or a little Buddha, whatever you want, but that feeling of gratitude and acceptance to me is important."

Hallelujah anyway.

In a final attempt to draw conclusions on the character of a man, we can do worse than to consider the opinion of his children grown. Better yet, we might observe their treatment of him when they are unaware of our prying eyes. This sort of behavior being potentially illegal and certainly creepy, we will settle for being quite innocently privy to the child's voice coming from a telephone.

In the case of Greg Brown, it was his daughter Constie, calling just as our interview began. Brown's cellular was in speakerphone mode, and although he stubbed away at the buttons with his meat-cutter fingers, he couldn't get it switched to a more private setting. I killed the tape recorder, so as not to capture the actual exchange, but the thing that struck me was the tone of Constie's voice. "Daddy," I heard her say, but it was not a frothy Daddy, not a little-girly "Daddy." No goobering, no giggling. Plain and simple warm affection. Honestly, I thought of whole-wheat bread, fresh on the sill. And I thought about my own life, and my own daughter, and what sort of person she might one day see me to be.

You don't marry thrice and live the road-dog life without ripple, and you figure Constie and her sisters know their father as a man of certain complications, but what a revelatory joy to hear that glow in her voice, in the way she said "Daddy." Spoken so, you figure the word strengthens the heart of a man, secondhand

and stuttering though it may be. Or especially so. You figure the shortcomings are no secret, the disappointments are duly noted, and still the scale tips to love. You figure the man has earned some redemption in this life, on this earth.

And that's really all he's looking for.

2006

P.S. I went home and I read Jude the Obscure. *Oof.*

KING PLEASURE

At times we are given to know that we are outside our territory: a Wisconsin boy, for instance, afoot in Oakdale, Tennessee, surprised by dogwoods blooming in April. I am standing on Piney Road, overlooking the river Sherwood Anderson called the Babahatchie. The spring sun is working the asphalt, loosening the scent of petroleum. It is a thick scent, molasses-brown and dumpy, the perfect base against which to draw in the fragrance of the dogwoods, like meringue over mud pie. Among the pines and kudzu trash, insects kite through the sunbeams like vigorous dust motes. The pitch of the land, imparted in this case by the nearby Cumberlands, feels exotic to a northwoods flatlander. I imagine things coming down from the hills.

I am trying to get a feel for this place, but I am also trying to get a feel for another time. A time when the valley below was chockablock with buildings. When young boys walked the streets in sandwich boards advertising shows at J. C. Alley's Opra House, when the beer at the Hole-in-the-Wall Saloon was chilled with ice cut from the river, when the vacant ridge along Piney Road was studded with houses. Oakdale was riding a boom in the early 1900s, stoked by the rails running the curve of the Babahatchie. The switching yards were filled with cars gathered for the 22-mile run up to Pilot Mountain. Built trackside, the YMCA hosted around 800 passengers per day and served 209,000 meals per year. A new train rolled through every three minutes. The railroad was its own sort of river.

In 1922, somewhere back up in the hills where the old-timers say the black folks lived, out of sight of the trains but within earshot of their rumble and whine, a boy was born to Mr. and Mrs. Butler Beeks. They named him Clarence.

Butler Beeks worked on the railroad, as did most Oakdale residents—black or white. He owned 47 acres back in the ridges, and he kept a garden. Sometimes, coming down the footpath, he carried produce for the market. The locals recall little Clarence tagging behind. They also recall that Butler unfailingly doffed his hat upon meeting a lady.

Guided by a local schoolteacher, I went back up Reynolds Road, where they say Clarence lived. Stood in the woods. There was no sign of a house. The sun cut through the trees all around. I was trying to think of this place at night, with maybe a whippoorwill calling, and young Clarence, six years old, waking upright (as he would tell it later) with a revelation that he was "the real savior of humanity."

Within the year, a great flood swept Oakdale. The theater was ruined. The bridge went down. Boxcars floated off the siding, the roundhouse was torn up, homes disappeared. When the water receded, it took the boom with it. The railroad never did come all the way back. During the boom, Oakdale reported some 3,500 citizens. Today there are about 300. You can trace the decline back to the Great Flood of 1929. And shortly thereafter—no one is clear on the details—this savior of humanity departed the region.

Afoot in the world of jazz, or bebop, or jive, I am outside my territory. I have an appreciation, not an understanding. I am underqualified to rank the who's who. I know from various sources that in November of 1951, Clarence Beeks came to the stage of the Apollo Theater in Harlem armed with lyrics written for James Moody's recording of the heretofore instrumental "I'm in the Mood for Love." To speak in the idiom, he broke the place up. Swinging his voice like a saxophone, he blew words like James

Moody blew notes, and when it was over, Clarence was declared winner of Amateur Night at the Apollo. In early 1952, Clarence recorded the tune—renaming it "Moody's Mood for Love"—and it hit No. 5 on the R&B charts. Also that year, *DownBeat* magazine named "Moody's Mood for Love" its Readers Poll Record of the Year. Clarence—having taken to calling himself "King Pleasure"— set off on tour, performing from the seat of a swiveling purple throne with a microphone incorporated into the armrest.

It should end there, on the upbeat.

The thing Clarence Beeks was doing, the singing like a saxophone, was known as *vocalese*. An evolution of the scat singing pioneered by Louis Armstrong in 1926, vocalese replaced the improvised, meaningless syllables of scat with fully realized lyrics written to mimic jazz solos note for note. The success of "Moody's Mood for Love" was definitive and established Beeks as a pioneer in the genre. It seems clear, however, that he was following in the steps of Eddie Jefferson, a former tap dancer from Pittsburgh.

According to an entry in Bill Milkowski's *Swing It! An Annotated History of Jive,* Jefferson was practicing vocalese as early as 1938, and replacing instrumental solos with lyrics in live sessions dated to 1949. According to several other sources, it was Jefferson who put the lyrics to "I'm in the Mood for Love." In *Swing It!,* Milkowski writes that Beeks saw Jefferson perform the song at the Cotton Club in Cincinnati just prior to Beeks's performance at the Apollo. In later years, Jefferson would say that Beeks "copped" the lyrics. According to liner notes written by Ira Gitler in 1991, Beeks gave credit to Jefferson for creating vocalese (Beeks favored the term *blowing*—as in, blowing through an instrument), but claimed the lyrics as his own. Beeks had another Top 5 hit in 1953 with "Red Top," and he kept recording into the early 1960s, but his acclaim was on the fade. When HiFi Jazz released his 1960 album *Golden Days,* Clarence wrote his own liner notes. He told the story of his being woke upright in Oakdale. As a result of the revelations of that time, he explained, he had formulated a philosophy of "Planetism." He called it the "ultimate 'ism,'" and while he felt the philosophy was incomplete, he deemed the "What I have found" important to humanity and worthy of enumeration, as follows:

1. That this is a charged-neutral material existence . . .

2. People are in ideal and physical metamorphosis (evolution) to a planet-satellite (moon)—the second Earth satellite . . .

3. People do not have to die. Life and death are matters of general adjustment (union) and maladjustment (separation) . . . All things come from "nothing" (space) . . . ALL things exist, live and react in relation [to] space.

By the mid-1960s, Clarence was living in California, and—again according to liner notes by Gitler—was sometimes "hostile" in phone conversations with friends. There were reports of him performing in Cincinnati as late as 1968, but when he died on March 21, 1981, he was living in Los Angeles. Quincy Jones reportedly paid for the funeral.

"As far as I know, I am the only child of my mother and father," says Constance Brewster, daughter of Clarence Beeks. We're speaking by phone—me in Wisconsin, she in Cincinnati. Constance says her mother and father separated before she was five. "He was very seldom around my supper table," she says. But she remembers him visiting. "He always brought me something I might like," she says. "Typewriters, bicycles, puppies." She giggles at the memory. Mostly though, she sounds cautious and weary. She feels her father and the family have been shorted. "We can listen to him on the radio now, singing the songs, knowing that the lyrics came from his brain, but yet everybody else takes credit for it. Even rap groups have sampled his stuff, or have used some of his lyrics. You have to work to make what you get, and you're supposed to be able to support your family and help them, and I'm sure that was his intention, but somehow it didn't fall that way. We're sittin' here broke and everyone else is livin' large."

Shortly before his death, Clarence Beeks asked Constance to bring him a copy of *Give Me the Night,* the George Benson album produced by Quincy Jones. "He liked this one particular song that he wanted to write lyrics to," says Constance. When Clarence discovered the album included a version of "Moody's Mood," he became upset. "He didn't know there was one of his songs on the album," she says. Eddie Jefferson is listed in the credits, but Constance objects: "There's no question about who wrote the lyrics—that came straight out of my dad's head. Out of his brain. Eddie Jefferson may have copied the style, lyrics, what have you, but that's about it. My dad wrote the lyrics. You can't take that away. He thought those up himself."

Eddie Jefferson won't be heard from. He died in 1979, shot down outside a Detroit music club. On *Golden Days,* the album through which Clarence proclaimed the ultimate 'ism,' Clarence obliquely offers: "I made this interpretation and developed Eddie's baby and delivered it to the public."

I ask Constance what she knows of Planetism. "I don't know what he was talking about with that," she says.

There are questions, as likely grown out of disappointment as deception. The purple throne is lost to history. Dogwoods bloom and fall. Having stood where he was born, it is tempting to riff on the otherworldly little boy, to extrapolate from his professed vision. But listening to Constance, I am reminded that sometimes he was simply Daddy. When I listen to *Moody's Mood for Love,* the 18-song Blue Note retrospective released in 1992, I hear a musician in complete coolheaded command of his instrument.

Steady in the steady parts, smooth in the smooth parts, and groovy when it counts. If he was troubled, or concerned with charged-neutral existence, it isn't evident in the bounce of "Jazz Jump" or the ha-ha-ha's of "Don't Get Scared." "Old Black Magic (Diaper Pin)" unfurls in a way that brings to mind a rippling satin ribbon. And perhaps I presume too much, but when he scats and yelps out the spider lines in "It Might as Well Be Spring," I recall the insects kiting through the sunlight up on the Piney Road ridge, and when I hear the opening lines of "Swan Blues," I think, That man was born hearing trains.

There are two versions of "Moody's Mood" included in the collection. Both are listed without credits, and in what appears to be yet another copyright-related move, under the original title "I'm in the Mood for Love." Pleasure utterly inhabits each version. There are a few rat-a-tat runs, a judicious smidge of vibrato here, a hip slur note there, a few skittery runs up and down the scale, but most of all, the feel that dominates is assuredness: He was at ease in the song.

All things exist, live, and react in relation to space. At times we are given to know that we are outside our territory. Clarence Beeks as King Pleasure—inside the song, living and reacting in relation to that musical space he understood so intuitively—was at home.

Back in Oakdale, there are flat spots carved into the hills where the boomtown houses once stood, and where, if you step to the edge, you can imagine how it might feel to be a boy looking down at the Babahatchie, ready to sing for the planet and all its satellites.

2003

P.S. This piece follows the Greg Brown piece by chance rather than chronology . . . I find it interesting that in both pieces I considered the singers in the context of "Daddy."

MOLLY AND THE HEYMAKERS

On a gray windy day in May 1991, I walked into a Kleenex box of a building on a discontinued farmstead in northern Wisconsin and got—as the dirt-track homeboys say—my doors blowed off. I had driven to Lenroot Township in Sawyer County at the behest of a magazine editor who had received a note claiming there was some band in Hayward that had people talking. *Molly & the Heymakers,* it said on the slip of paper. We were ignorant, and figured there was polka involved.

Five minutes after I stepped through the door of that little building my misconceptions had been given a spanking and were fading in the rearview mirror as the band speed-shifted through "Jimmy McCarthy's Truck." I was hooked at the first twangy lick. When the drums kicked in, my heart leapt. And when Molly Scheer sang the first verse, I wanted to stand right up and testify:

It was an old red flatbed '69 Ford
With lots of dents and rust around the doors
It was an ugly thing, but at seventeen it gave us wings
Ridin' around in Jimmy McCarthy's truck

Man, I was Jimmy.

The day I met them, Molly & the Heymakers were on their way. They had just signed a two-album contract with Warner Brothers. Their first single, "Chasin' Something Called Love," had recently broken into the Top 40. The video accompanying the song was a top 10 favorite on Country Music Television (CMT) and played heavily on The Nashville Network (TNN). A follow-up video for "Mountain of Love" crossed over from CMT and TNN to VH1. The band was making trips to Tennessee to appear on *Nashville Now* and *Crook and Chase,* and they were getting requests to open shows for Alabama, Sawyer Brown, Charlie Daniels, Travis Tritt, and the Judds. In a genre dominated by southerners and westerners, they were northerners headed for the big time.

They made it, too. Had a taste. But after "Big Bad Love," Molly & the Heymakers never made another video. Their next single didn't chart. You'd see them out there, still touring, playing the clubs and festivals and even shows in Europe, but you never heard their songs on the radio anymore. And then one day you heard someone say, *Whatever happened to . . . ?*

The Heymakers might never have happened at all if not for the tourist industry. In the early 1980s, guitarist Andy Dee was in a weekend band playing the resort circuit of northern Minnesota and Wisconsin when Molly—visiting the area with her husband's lumberjack show—appeared with a fiddle and sat in. "She kept showing up and everyone loved her," says Dee, "so she became part of the band." Andy, however, would shortly commit career whiplash, departing for Hawaii, where he spent three years pursuing a master's degree in zoology. By 1986 his studies were complete, but he missed music desperately.

Molly was now fronting the house band at a ski lodge in Cable, and Andy flew home to join up. After a lineup change, the band began playing more outside dates, and a Minneapolis booking agent suggested they call themselves Molly & the Haymakers. They liked the name, but decided to change the first "a" to an "e." It was a neat little twist, with one drawback: "It was," says Andy ruefully, "misspelled a lot."

◆ ◆ ◆

By 1987, the band (with original members Dave Berrard, Tom Blaine, and drummer "Solid" Joe Lindzius) was playing small bars and private parties in northern Wisconsin. "Then we started to get gigs in the Twin Cities," says Andy. "We would drive over and play for nothing, basically, just to get an opening set at a decent club." The Heymakers opened for Three Dog Night in Eau Claire and Johnny Rivers in Niagara. By now they were writing and performing original material. They recorded some of the songs on a homemade cassette, and, in Andy Dee's words, "handed 'em out like business cards."

Fans of chaos theory frequently cite the butterfly effect, in which meteorologist Edward Lorenz postulated that the flap of a butterfly's wings in Brazil can—given time—trigger a tornado in Texas. What happened to the Heymakers might be referred to as the cassette effect. The night the Heymakers opened for Rivers in Niagara, a drummer named Keith Edwards caught the show and grabbed one of their cassettes. That cassette made its way to a producer named Paul Worley, who was in charge of one of the top studios in Nashville. After Worley listened to the tape, he tracked down Molly and invited her to bring the band to Tennessee for a showcase. Molly turned the tables, convincing Worley to come north and observe the band in its own element, playing Bunkers, a biker bar in St. Paul. Worley loved the show, and signed Molly to a music publishing deal. The deal made news in Nashville, partly because of the unusual fact that Molly was from rural Wisconsin. Soon talent scouts were regulars in the Bunkers audience. Things moved fast. "It was like bam, bam, bam," says Andy Dee. "Publishing, record label, then national bookings." In a trice, the band had signed a two-album deal and was in a Nashville recording studio. The cassette effect had triggered a string of fortuitous chaos. But somewhere, less benevolent breezes were stirring.

As financial writers are prone to say these days, *full disclosure:* I once pulled a brief stint as a Heymakers roadie. The band was playing a string of European country music festivals and needed help with the luggage. I was hanging out in England, so I grabbed a train through the Chunnel and met the band in Worb, Switzerland. I had perfected the roadie look: baggy shorts, shaggy head, black T-shirt, gaffer's tape on my belt, and a fanny pack full of Sharpies. My abilities, however, were pretty much limited to the category of Can Lift Things. When Andy broke a string midshow, I fumbled in a box for two songs before I found the correct replacement (I'd push the little envelopes to the edge of the stage lights and Andy—still playing—would shake his head). When one of the stagehands realized I didn't know how to string a guitar, she strung it herself and handed it back like I was a very special child. I ran out onstage all hunched over like roadies do and stuck the guitar in its stand, but not before taping a note to it that said, *"Not tuned!"*

The day before I headed back to England, a local promoter took us to the top of a cathedral in Geneva. As we looked over the ancient city, Andy marveled gratefully that a guy could ride a guitar all the way from Hayward, Wisconsin, to Switzerland. Earlier in the day, I had opened the door to our hotel room and caught him playing scales on that same guitar. I saw a guy whose abilities had earned him record deals, bright lights, and big stages, still doing his homework. I tell you these things up front, so that you know my sentiments: I wish things had gone better for Molly & the Heymakers.

The trouble with the question *"Whatever happened to . . . ?"* is that the answer lies in an endless backtrack from the present, through thousands of miles and hundreds of shows, all manner of breaks and dead-ends. Furthermore, the story is neither rare nor unique nor limited to artists. Every day plumbers, nurses, gardeners, and social workers pay dues on dreams bound to be thwarted by an infinity of slippery variables. It just so happens that when your workplace is a stage, the audience eventually looks up and notices that you've gone.

Country music is notoriously cyclical, and Molly & the Heymakers emerged in the nascent flush of the biggest upturn ever. Garth Brooks was parlaying his aw-shucks demeanor and rock-show pyrotechnics into the monster that would require no other name than *Garth*. His counterpart in the one-name fame-stakes, Reba McEntire, was revolutionizing the business, becoming her own industry, right down to the construction of a personal multistory office complex destined to kick-start the transformation of Nashville's Music Row from sleepy street to hyperbolic glass and marble canyonette.

In general, this was all good news. The younger, more suburban fans attracted by Garth's laser show were receptive to country music that went beyond the traditional tear-in-your-beer weepers or the leisure suit sounds of the late 1970s and early 1980s, and Nashville was hungry to capitalize on the new market. Fresh acts were in high demand, and the Heymakers fit the bill. They were country—Molly's fiddle and Andy's big guitar twang established that, and songs about boys in trucks didn't hurt—but they were also young and hip. Molly's fiddle was blood red and electric, and for all his musicianship, Andy was a tongue-in-cheek whirligig, tossing his guitar, leaping off the drum riser, kicking his lap steel flat after a tearaway solo, then stopping to stand ramrod straight while reciting the Scout's Pledge. His undergraduate training as a graphic artist showed in his stage outfits, including an orange jumpsuit plastered with snapshots of stuffed fish and a vest made from a velvet Elvis painting. For her part, Molly was prone to combining sequins, lace-up boots, gauze skirts, and western-cut jackets for a look best described as bohemian lumberjill chic. When Andy stopped the show to invoke Hayward's National Freshwater Fishing Hall of Fame and introduce Molly as "the Muskie Queen, the Temptress of Trout, the Wahini of Walleye," Molly would step forward with a fixed pageant smile, do her best campy parade wave, and, as she whipped her fiddle bow into the next number, confide, "Yes, ladies and gentlemen, it's all in the wrist." If you went to a Heymakers show you got rock-solid music, but you also had *fun*. The music—especially the original material—was worthy of a straight listen, but if you wanted to whoop it up and boot scoot, that'd work too.

The big breaks came, *bam, bam, bam.* The break*down* came in dribs and drabs.

The mainstream country music boom that caught the Heymakers in its updraft spawned a countermovement of fans and artists in a genre that came to be called alternative (or "alt") country. With influences ranging from punk rock to folk ballads, alt-country didn't always sound specifically "country," but its practitioners drew deeply on a loosely defined assortment of traditional influences. Above all, they eschewed the gloss and pop personified by Garth and Reba. Early on, the Heymakers sparked interest in the alt-crowd, but when they showed signs of success, the hipsters began second-guessing. "We were too mainstream," says Andy. In particular, critics targeted their lighthearted stage presence. Molly stuck to her guns. "My father was a brilliant musician," she says. "He was also a performer, and the one thing he instilled in me is, you have to have a show. Even if it means wearing a hat and shirt so that the lights reflect. It is a visual world."

Hipsters notwithstanding, the Heymakers' show put people on the dance floor. But even this wasn't enough. In 1992, Billy Ray Cyrus released "Achy Breaky Heart," and everybody and their grandma bought a cowboy hat and started line dancing. "You'd play the last note in the set and *bam!* The DJ would be pumping records twice as loud as the band, and everyone would be out there with their thumbs in their pants, wiggling their asses and clicking their heels," recalls Andy. "The first time I saw that happen, I turned to the band and said, 'That is the end of cool country music—it is now officially dorky.' And I was right. It became all about line dancing and not about music." Too fun for alt-country and too offbeat for the "Achy Breaky" crowd, the Heymakers wound up somewhere in the middle.

The initial success of their singles and videos gave the Heymakers that invaluable Music City commodity, *buzz.* They were on the radio. They were on television. The album was recorded and ready for release. Then the second single didn't do as well as the first, and the promotions people got nervous. "They listened to the album and said they didn't hear a hit," says Andy. "So they sent us back in the studio to record three more songs." The promotions people still didn't hear a hit. A week before the album was supposed to be released, the label pulled it.

A new producer was procured, and the band recorded five more songs, including "Mountain of Love." "The video did well," says Andy, "but the single started hot and just fizzled." In the meantime, the label was being torn apart by a sexual harassment suit. People were being laid off. Bands were being let go. The label was having trouble generating hits for stalwarts like Randy Travis, never mind upstarts like the Heymakers. Seeing the writing on the wall, Molly and Andy cut themselves loose. "We collected the advance on the second album and parted ways," says Andy.

Thanks to a widespread, loyal fan base—and in no small part due to their sometimes maligned live show—the band was able to keep on keepin' on, but the lights were never again quite as bright. They produced a couple of new albums in a modest garage-sized studio across the yard from the tiny studio where it all began, and Molly continued to prospect for a deal. "We were still doing a lot of work in Europe, still making a living, but I could see that Nashville had become a different ball game," she says. Time was passing. Andy got married, and at 40, Molly was rethinking her priorities. "When you're hot, you're hot," she says with a wry grin. "And then all of a sudden you are changing clothes in a porta-potty at some festival, and it just hits you . . . this is really not a business to grow gracefully old in."

In 1997, Molly Scheer and Andy Dee dissolved their partnership. "In hindsight," says Andy, "we probably should have hung it up two or three years earlier."

◆ ◆ ◆

The postscript has its rough patches (recently divorced, Molly has gone back to her father's surname and is now Molly Otis; Andy's daughter Lily, born with Down syndrome, has had several heart surgeries), but if you're looking for some grim has-been tragedy, you won't find it here. Andy's distinctive big-note twang and virtuoso lap steel still earn him regular work in Minneapolis studios, where he has contributed to major label sessions for the Proclaimers, Jonny Lang, and Bobby Vee. He currently lives in Savage, Minnesota, and spends the bulk of his time in his basement studio producing music for a variety of projects: the film score for the Sundance award–winning film *Quick Stop,* a series of commercials for the Chipotle Restaurant chain, ads for United Airlines, Best Buy, Coke, L. L. Bean, John Deere, and Arctic Cat. "And Johnsonville brats!" he jokes. "Yay, Wisconsin!" He is working on a collection of unreleased Heymaker recordings and still plays a few live engagements. "It's all pretty much local," he says. "Once in a while I go to Duluth."

And Molly? "I pretty much quit playing music altogether except for the symphony up in Ashland," she says. "It's a weird thing when you realize you are 40 and basically unhireable. I didn't have any skills besides being the lead singer in a band." After teaching herself to paint trompe l'oeil designs on furniture, she found she could sell enough of the pieces to sustain her own small shop. The store did well, surprising her. Next she renovated an old 7,000-square-foot building in downtown Hayward and opened the Pavilion, a store carrying an eclectic mix of art, homeware, gardenware, and music.

Once the Pavilion was up and running, Molly opened Madeline's, a coffeehouse-style restaurant. "Madeline's and the Pavilion are composites of all the hip little spots I saw when I was traveling the world in the band," she explains. In the evenings, Madeline's hosts poetry readings, foreign film showings, open mike nights, and live music—sometimes including the proprietor. "It's the most fun I have all week," says Molly. "I really don't do originals anymore. Just fun music."

As of this year, Molly Otis has put her restaurant up for sale. She is contemplating a move. She rarely gets the Heymaker question anymore. For a while the reactions to her musical success made her uncomfortable. "People said I was a bad mother because I was on the road," she says. "We went from being the darlings of the Minneapolis press to being slammed as sellouts. People see you on TV and they don't realize that you got $100 to drive 16 hours to Nashville. Friendships suffered. When we got the record deal I called my mom and realized I had no one else to call. But I look back on it with a smile. I delight in the rare experiences I had and the people I worked with and what we did. I went places I never would have gone. I saw a lot of people get bitter, and I didn't want to get trapped in that."

Andy feels the same. "Being from up in the woods, we had the deck stacked against us in a few ways . . . it helped with our image to a point, but it wasn't an image the good old boys could latch onto down South. We had a lot of luck. We got our songs on the radio and got to be on TV. We got to play big shows and tour the country in a big bus."

Rounder Records still carries *Big Things,* the album Molly and Andy produced in the wake of the Warner debacle. The last track on the album, "Nice Girls Finish Last," was written by Molly and features Andy's signature guitar work. Some 30 seconds after the last note fades to silence, Andy Dee's voice pops out of the speakers. He's clowning, overenunciating like a goofily manic disc jockey as he hollers, *"Thank you very much, everybody!"*

It's all that's left to say.

EARLY 2000s

P.S. These days Molly lives in Bayfield, Wisconsin, plays regularly at the Lake Superior Big Top Chautauqua, and writes songs for a music publisher. Andy continues to record, produce, and play. Lily is thriving. In a development none of us foresaw, Andy and Molly appear regularly with a band called the Long Beds, fronted by a guy who was never much of a roadie but has learned to string his own guitar.

LETTER TO LIGHTNIN' HOPKINS

I wrote this shortly after I was married. While my children learned their share of nursery rhymes, I saw no harm in starting them equally early on other durable genres.

Dear Lightnin' Hopkins:

There's a new girl in my life, and this time it's serious, because she is four years old and I have married her mama and as such I will be held at least partially responsible for the vagaries—bent or beautiful—in the character she becomes. I work at home, where she is forever underfoot because we are strict and forbid her to work the rodeo circuit or attend raves at the gravel pit. Once when I was slumped at the keyboard in my usual under-productive funk with the CD player locked on shuffle, she heard you singing "Shaggy Dad" at which point she ditched her stuffed horse and entered the room spinning and juking like a ballerina with an affliction of trick knees. She was the picture of delight.

I have done a little rummaging around and understand the archival purists hardly rank "Shaggy Dad" among your finest, but the pressure is off, because I'm no purist. Not that I object to purism. While in conversation with this overeducated friend of mine a few years back I was moved to address the candied decline of mainstream country music into neutered theraspeak, but paused to preface my jeremiad by saying I didn't want to sound elitist. My friend stopped me cold: "I stopped apologizing for being an elitist a long time ago." That tempered my thinking some and left me feeling like a lumpen doofus. Later, however, that same friend decreed, "There are no guilty pleasures—only *pleasures.*" Which frees me to say that "Shaggy Dad" is, and always will be, my favorite Lightnin' Hopkins song, even after this little girl breaks my heart, which is what all little girls are fixing to do.

On October 25, 1990, Townes Van Zandt played a solo show at the Quasimodo Club in Berlin. Four numbers in, he said, "This is a Lightnin' Hopkins song." Then he sang "Short-Haired Woman Blues." A Dutch label released a recording of the show on an album called *Rain on a Conga Drum,* and I figure when I played it that's the first I ever heard your name. By the mid-'90s Townes Van Zandt had drawn me deep into the alt-country movement, and I noticed a lot of the artists in *No Depression* magazine name-checked you. So I took a shot and ordered *The Very Best of Lightnin' Hopkins.* One album. That's it. Rated, furthermore, by *All Music Guide* as "largely nonessential." Frankly, you have better fans. Aficionados more qualified to parse your oeuvre.

But sir, you should see that little girl dance.

She'll ask for you, Mr. Hopkins. Ask for you by name. She is a slender, blonde, blue-eyed little girl, and she will appear in my doorway and say, "Can you play Lightnin' Hopkins?" She is precise about dropping the 'g.' You don't turn your back on a request like that, not with the world in the state it is. Soon enough, I will be saying things like, "Sweetie, in my day good girls were happy with a nice nipple ring." I find the CD, place it in the tray, advance to track 12, and push *Play.*

Those first guitar notes are nimble and lighthearted. She twitches in place, arms at *bras au repos,* just like the lady in the leotard taught her at the YMCA. Then the bass and snare get to spanking along, and she begins to spin, undulating her arms and weaving her feet in an imitation of I believe *chaines* or *chasse,* or some approximate amalgamation. Sometimes she reaches for my hands and my heart soars, but not my feet. I am an arrhythmic clod, but the trombone bops and grooves like a light-footed fat man, giving us license to goof, and we do the Saint Vitus polka. You ease through the lyrics with tossed-off panache, deceiving us into thinking we can do the same. Mostly we lag and mumble, but come in strong for every *Shaggy Dad. "Jumped on a alligator,"* you sing, *"thought it was a horse,"* and she laughs and laughs. *"Got a good reputation,"* you sing, *"but the man is bad,"* and I look in her blue eyes and think, *Lord, I hope that one registers.*

Somewhere along the line, Mr. Hopkins, I'm gonna steer her wrong. Already have. "Who's your favorite Delta blues singer?" I ask. "Lightnin' Hopkins!" she cheers, just the way I taught her. I am an idiot, of course, because you were not a Delta bluesman per se, you were from Texas, and you played country blues. Although the *Very Best Of* liner notes claim your style includes a touch of the delta. I don't know. I am not well-versed in pedigree. From Leadbelly to you, I can't recite all the *begats.* I just look at that little girl dancing to the lope of a song dismissed in the aforementioned liner notes as *"more cultural artifact . . . than solid blues,"* and, knowing we must eventually release her into the pernicious maelstrom, I long that she might safely navigate a stretch of time, maybe all through her teens and well into womanhood, where she doesn't listen to that song at all—forgets about it, even—and then one day it will play out of some speaker or holographic listening device, and she will feel the vestigial stirrings of a tiny dancer. She will feel joy and yearning for the resurrection of lost days, and she shall have them, thanks to a song.

Her daddy is a tall man, Lightnin'. That's where she got the legs. From her mama, the blond hair and eyes like clear sky. I am a late arrival. I bring her boogie and blues, courtesy of you.

With a song in my heart,
Michael "Slow Bones" Perry

2005

THE POWER AND THE GLORY

Ryan Hall will be happy with second place. In his prayers, he thinks of entering Heaven, and imagines running through the gates as if into a great stadium filled with people raising a joyful noise. He hopes to be just off the shoulder of the leader, but he won't attempt a late kick. "The goal of my life," he says, "is just to follow in the footsteps of Jesus as closely as I can."

At the risk of committing light blasphemy, let it be said the Son of God may want a new pair of shoes. Not only did Hall win the US Olympic Marathon Trials, he was the fastest qualifier in American history, taming a tough New York City course in a Trials-record 2:09:02. It was only his second race at the distance; his first was the 2007 Flora London Marathon, where his 2:08:24 was the fastest debut by an American. Returning to London in 2008, he ran 2:06:17, breaking his own record for the fastest marathon ever run by an American-born citizen. Three marathons, three benchmarks. When Ryan Hall toes the starting line in Beijing, he will be operating at a level of possibility not seen since the days of Alberto Salazar.

Even so, it's hard to imagine a race that can supplant the memory of Hall's win at the Trials. It wasn't so much the record broken as the galvanizing manner in which he broke it, dusting an all-star pack and covering the final miles less like a marathoner than an amped-up slugger circling the bases after a walk-off homer. But then, in this glorious hour, the darkest news: 20 miles back, his friend and fellow competitor Ryan Shay had fallen dead. Just four months earlier, Hall's wife, Sara, had served as bridesmaid when their mutual friend Alicia Craig married Shay. All four were record-breaking distance runners with Olympic dreams.

A year has nearly passed, and of the four, only Hall is set to run beneath the rings. How will he approach the moment? The story will be variously framed: The athlete running for the memory of a fellow racer, the fallen friend, the grieving family; the underperformer who switched genres and scorched his way into history; the man caught in a dialectic in which his most transcendent moment is forever tethered to grim mortality.

Hall prefers another story. The *only* story, he says; the one that helps us understand why he might remain modest in triumph and strong in tragedy. He calls it the greatest story ever told.

It's Sunday morning, and Ryan Hall is late for church. This is not to imply that Hall is slothful. Quite the opposite. He rose at dawn. For a 15-mile run. Under normal circumstances he knocks that distance down with time to spare before services commence. But this morning he was running in the company of an NBC television crew, and they needed B-roll and interview footage. By the time it was in the can, the Summit Christian Fellowship church choir had taken hymnals in hand. They are currently in full throat, accompanied by electric bass and a drummer on a trap set. The words to the hymns, superimposed over scenes of ocean waves and sunsets, are projected on two pull-down screens flanking the riser. As the verses flip by, the congregation—60 or so people seated in a room decorated with plastic ivy, artificial Christmas trees, and strings of white lights—sings along. As the last hymn prior to worship builds to a crescendo, two men stationed on opposite sides of the room fire handheld confetti cannons. The final notes of praise rise through a powdered rainbow tumbling down.

The church is located across from the Big Bear Disposal Site & Recycling Center. Big Bear Lake, California, is an enclave of the sort and size that operates at the tipping point between the American small town as defined by central casting (old-timers staking out well-worn counter seats at the Teddy Bear Restaurant) and a resort town developed to snag outsiders (Starbucks, faux Alpine lodges, a go-cart course). Set far away from the rest of the world in the San Bernardino Mountains (at roughly the same elevation as that crucible of marathoning, Kenya's Great Rift Valley), it can be fairly characterized as sleepy on an off-season Sunday morning, and anything but when the ski-booted masses descend at peak time. Today is one of the quiet Sundays. The spring sun has baked a pitchy scent from the needles fallen beneath the tall pines surrounding the church, and the pickups and minivans of the families within sit on the asphalt lot outside. The church building itself is a humble one-story structure painted pale green—you might miss it for what it is should you fail to spot a Calvary's trio of small crosses planted near the entrance. There is another even smaller cross visible just below the peak of the roof. Before you see either of these, you will probably see the white banner tacked to the siding. In blue letters it reads, "Run, Ryan, Run!"

Big Bear Lake is out there, twinkling in the sun, penned in by a dam on one end, and by mountains to either side. If you drive up from San Bernardino, you'll want to dose on Dramamine for the switchbacks on Highway 18. The climb terminates in a fork at the dam where Highway 18 splits to run the south shore, Highway 38 the north. Toward the far end of the lake, a bridge called the Stansfield Cutoff reunites the roads, enclosing the water in a 15-mile loop. In a sense that loop is Ryan Hall's road to Damascus, where the Bible tells us the Christian-killer Saul of Tarsus pulled a spiritual U-turn and became the loyal Apostle Paul. For purposes of conversion, the Lord knocked Saul flat and struck him blind. Happily in Hall's case, he settled for just tuckering the boy out some.

"In eighth grade I was kind of at a crossroads in my life," says Hall. You're about to roll your eyes, looking at this pure-faced blue-eyed 25-year-old with the blond hair, and then he smiles and adds, "I didn't realize it at the time, you know." Hall speaks in a southern California patois that, accurately or not, will remind a Midwesterner of surfboards. His sentences are heavily leavened with "like" and he will deploy "gnarly" as an adjective without irony. His gaze is considerate and thoughtful, and apparently incapable of guile. But do not think *pushover*—he emanates the steadfast resolve of the true believer. If by way of introduction you reveal that you do not believe as he believes, his countenance remains warm and open, but you will catch just a shade of the patient indulgence believers reserve for those yet a-wandering.

"My parents were strong Christians," he continues. "I definitely believed, but I wasn't really strongly pursuing my faith. I was playing baseball, basketball, football—I was into, like, the cool crowd at school. And then one day traveling down the mountain to a basketball game, I got this random—I describe it as a vision, but you could call it an idea, whatever—this thing pops into my mind where I am looking out at Big Bear Lake, and I think, well, it would be a great thing for me to try and run around that."

It's tough to put this in context now, what with the mind-bending marathon times in the books and Beijing right around the corner. But Hall wants you to understand that the power of the vision lay partially in the fact that he was not being asked to do something to which he seemed naturally inclined. "I never really had any interest in running. Like, in middle school, whenever they made us run the mile, I'd complain just like everyone else. But at that moment it became something that was very captivating . . . it really grabbed me."

By now, of course, the story about the kid who circumnavigated Big Bear Lake in basketball shoes has become central to the Ryan Hall legend. He ran the route with his father, Mickey. Mickey says they made one stop in 15 miles, and he knew already the boy had something special. The kid was worn out at the end, but back home while unlacing his shoes, Ryan says he too knew this was more than a one-off stunt. "At that point, the trajectory of my life completely changed. All of a sudden I stopped doing baseball, basketball, and football, and started running full-time." And somewhere out on that loop, something else alchemized: "It was at that point that Jesus really became my best friend. That's when our relationship took off . . . and it was a direct result of him bringing running into my life."

At Summit Christian Fellowship, the people are praying. The highest-profile congregant has yet to present—he is re-creating that famous day for the cameras—but the flock understands what might be keeping him. After all, they are the ones who hung the banner. They know: God told Ryan to run.

Surely our feelings regarding athletes who choose to bring their faith to the field reflect the state of our own souls. Fellow believers will likely rejoice at God's word made manifest in the form of peak performance; nonbelievers will dismiss the testimony at best, deride it at worst. Ryan Hall believes he was chosen by God to run for God. One of Hall's favorite Bible verses—the one he scribbled on the autographed poster just inside the door of the Teddy Bear Restaurant in Big Bear Lake—is from the book of Isaiah. *Those who wait on the Lord, will run and not get tired.* The Lord has taught Hall not to overlook that key word: *wait.* The divine plan doesn't always run parallel to mortal hopes and dreams.

Consider Ryan Hall's earthly father. Mickey Hall is trim but solid. He is sitting midway up the aisle at Summit Christian Fellowship, and the hand he drapes across his Bible could swing a big hammer easy. In fact, he grew up framing houses for his father. Mickey's father drove the crew hard. "Head down, butt up!" he would say. "If you're not in that position, you're not making money." By age 42, Mickey's dad had enough scratch to retire, and "Head down, butt up!" had become the family motto.

If ever a man had the makings of a stage father of the first degree, it would be Mickey Hall. Ultracompetitive ("Maybe what you would call overcompetitive . . . I wouldn't let my grandmother beat me in a game of cards!"), drafted as a pitcher by the Baltimore Orioles in his first year of college, and given to obsessive use of a stopwatch (long before he was calling splits for Ryan on the track, Mickey would time the boy and his four siblings as they cut and split firewood), you might anticipate his reaction when he took his son for a run one day and discovered that his progeny was a prodigy.

You'd be wrong. "I tried to convince him to play baseball," Mickey says, laughing. "He could really throw!" But Ryan wanted to run. So Mickey stopped coaching baseball and started a track program (Big Bear had no track or cross-country team)—and began to deploy that stopwatch the way God intended.

Fraught waters, the whole father-as-coach thing. But Mickey has never forgotten the backstop his father built in the backyard when he was 11. "I would go out and throw half an hour every day at that thing," says Mickey, and he wound up getting his shot at the bigs. *Butt up, head down,* yes, but the marvelous thing, Mickey says, is that his dad always assigned work and play equal par. He put down the hammer and took the kids to the beach for volleyball. He taught them to surf and kicked Mickey loose of the construction crew so he could make baseball practice. When Ryan Hall tells the story of the firewood and the stopwatch, the smile on his face tells you the memory is not Dickensian. It is more "can-do" Bobbsey Twins. And it drives him still.

God may call you to run, but that doesn't mean you're on the fast track. You're the man, God told Moses, then sent him off on a four-decade detour. So even in Hall's immediate and revelatory promise as a runner, his father saw the potential for trouble.

"As a tiny ninth-grader competing against juniors and seniors he ran 4:35 in the mile," says Mickey. "I never had to push him. If anything, when Susie and I had to discipline him, we'd threaten to take away his training time." Mickey spent more time riding the brakes than cracking the whip. "I was with him for every workout in high school, and my tendency is to go too hard. So when he would go too hard, I would say, 'Whoa, we're done,' and he'd say, 'No, Dad, I can do more,' and I'd say, 'I know you can—you're not.'" Mickey Hall's fastball was clocking 90 miles per hour when his college coach asked him to pitch three innings of a preseason game. At the end of three, the score was tied zero-zero. The coach asked him to pitch one more. Still zero-zero. One more, said the coach. And back in he went, *head down, butt up,* inning after inning in a meaningless game until the ninth when his shoulder went *pop!* and the Orioles flew away forever.

Under his father's guidance, Ryan won four individual state titles in high school and ran a state-record time (4:02) for 1,600 meters. The recruiters were circling, and after much prayer, Ryan felt God directing him to Stanford. God also decided it was time to give Ryan a little taste of Job. Before preseason camp even began, he suffered an iliotibial-band injury. "From the moment I started at Stanford, I was off my game," he says now. "I was struggling with school, I was struggling with my running. I'd wake up in the morning with this heavy burden feeling, like *uhhhh, things are not what I had pictured.*" He slept poorly, ate poorly, and gained 10 pounds. In the absence of his father's governing hand and despite the advice of his college coach, he treated recovery runs as one more chance to hammer. Midway through his sophomore year, he was a bona fide flop. He abandoned Stanford for a quarter and returned home. He figured running the familiar roads would help him get things sorted. Help him recover the groove.

It turned out quite the opposite. "I got more depressed. I remember waking up in the morning, trying to go for a run this one day, it was snowing outside, and I just could not get myself out of bed. Went out, and was trying to, like, just do a short, easy run. And I jog, like, half a mile and I start walking. And I just walked home, 'cause my spirit was just crushed. Because I wasn't running well, I didn't see myself as having much worth."

This time there was no Road to Damascus moment. No blinding revelation. Hall gave himself over to prayer and pondering. "I realized the only things that were going well in college were my relationship with my girlfriend and my relationship with the Lord," says Hall, who had begun dating champion miler Sara Bei and befriended a circle of like-minded believers through his involvement in the Stanford chapter of Athletes in Action. "I decided that God had called me to go to Stanford." He returned to the university. "I was no longer a runner who happens to be a Christian," he says. "I was a Christian who happens to run."

Things didn't instantly change. "I still had a subpar track season that year," says Hall, who cites the end of his 2004 Olympic dreams as a low point. "But I was happy. I knew I was where I was supposed to be, and finally got to a point where I really enjoyed my time up at Stanford." Before he graduated in 2006, he'd won an NCAA championship at 5,000 meters, led Stanford to a team cross-country title, and married Bei. Things were looking up.

Today at Summit Christian Fellowship, the pastor isn't in the pulpit. He has given the microphone over to his wife and left for the parsonage, where he's washing lettuce and chopping chicken salad. It is Mother's Day, and at the end of the service, the pastor and several male parishioners will serve a luncheon to honor the mothers in their midst—Ryan Hall's mother included. The Hall family work ethic and competitive genetics may be patrilineal, but it was Susie who led Mickey Hall—and thus the rest of the Hall family—to Jesus. Mickey was an atheist in flip-flops when he followed Susie to church one day. Took a while, but in the process of writing a college paper about why the Bible was hoo-hah, he wound up a believer. And when Susie began volunteering on behalf of disabled children, Mickey noticed. In fact, when you sort out the chronology, you discover that Mickey turned down cash from the Orioles *before* his injury. He had seen the joy in Susie's service, he says, and he was already doubting the little white ball could match that. Now he has been working 21 years as a special-education teacher, and if you want to see his face light up, cut the track talk and ask about those students of his.

Mickey Hall has watched friends thrive in the big leagues. But when he recounts his baseball stories, there is no trace of *I coulda been a contender.* He revels in the telling. You look at him now worshipping beside the wife who showed him another way, and you see there is no room for regret in the joy. He is fond of quoting 1 Corinthians: *Run the race in such a way that you might win.* Compete with all your heart, he tells his children, Ryan included. "But don't make it bigger than it is—it's just a sport."

A woman makes her way to the front of the church. She has asked that the congregation pray over her. There is trouble on her face, tears coming down. From her modest podium, the pastor's wife calls on the Lord, and several parishioners close around the woman, some praying with a palm raised to heaven, others laying their hands on the petitioner. Somewhere amid the supplication, Ryan Hall quietly seats himself in the back row.

Hall doesn't take missing church lightly, but with his training and travel, absenteeism has become an occupational hazard. This has led him to examine the life of Brother Lawrence, a 17th-century Carmelite monk who taught that godly people should weave worship into work. "Brother Lawrence was one of the guys who pioneered that thought about doing every single little thing for the Lord and staying connected with him throughout the day in prayer," says Hall, who often listens to an audio version of the Bible while driving, or on his iPod while running. "Rather than study the Bible at some appointed hour, I try to make worship much more just a natural flow and part of my day," he says. "A big challenge for me is to *pray without ceasing* as the Bible tells us. So I pray when I am out running. Or doing dishes. When my mind is wandering, I try and hone it back into praying. I'm not very good at it yet."

Brother Lawrence also preached Christlike humility and warned of the consequences of pride. How does Hall reconcile these lessons when his job requires crushing the competition? "There's obviously a gray area," he says. "You gotta have confidence. The question is, what are you putting your confidence in: your own ability? And what do you believe about your ability? Do you believe you've done something to deserve it? Or is it a gift? I believe I have a gift from God. But then I also have to train really, really hard. So I see it as being a good steward of the gift God's given me . . . it's my obligation to God to develop this talent the best I can. So, I try and make that my focus rather than wanting to beat people. Not that it's not fun to win, because it is.

"I think part of it too is just being content with whatever the Lord has for my life."

But whither motivation? If all outcomes—win, place, or no-show—are God's will, does Hall have permission to lose? "I don't know," says Hall, after some thought. "I don't have all my theology figured out. I don't know if God has someone in mind to win the Olympic Marathon either. Only one guy can win that race, and everyone in that race wants to win and it's their dream to win, so what does that mean for the rest of us who don't win? The 99.9 percent of us who will never get a gold medal in the Olympics? Does that mean that we're all failures, and that all the training we did our whole life building up to it was a waste? Definitely not."

In the course of her homily, the pastor's wife reveals that she will be traveling to Beijing to see Ryan run. She does not want to go to China, she says. She has been telling the Lord so. But the Lord does everything for a purpose, she says, and somewhere in China that purpose will be revealed. Hall listens impassively but attentively. Wearing khaki cargo shorts and an Asics T-shirt, he looks preternaturally fine-tuned, the way all athletes do when at rest among the shlubby rest of us. Every move is a gesture of economy. His hand rests on his Bible, and his Bible rests across his right thigh. There is no dust on Ryan Hall's Bible. It is hardly tattered, but the gilding on the pages is scored and worn. When he opens it to follow the sermon, it falls open easily to reveal well-thumbed page corners and verses underlined in pen. This Bible is not a prop. You can see him turning to it again and again. When racing for Heaven, one must train to the finish.

"I don't think I have an exact point in my life when I accepted Christ," says Hall. "I can remember doing it—you know, as a kid—over and over again 'cause I was kind of afraid the first time didn't count or whatever. I wanted to make sure I was covered. What I have learned as I have gotten older is that it's such a daily thing. It's not a one-time decision and that seals the deal. It says in the Bible to work out your salvation *daily* with fear and trembling . . . it's a long journey and it's not like you instantly get to this holy status. I am very much still in process, as I think all Christians are. *All* people are, really . . . we're all still growing."

When the service concludes, everyone makes their way across the church parking lot to the parsonage, where tables have been set beneath the shade of the pine trees. Ryan sits next to his father, and the resemblance is strongest when the two men smile in unison. Their upper lips peel back to reveal a generous set of incisors, and you think of Gary Busey minus all the crazy.

Big Bear Lake has always turned out for ball games, not for track meets. In fact, when Hall won his state cross-country titles, he wasn't eligible for a letter because there was no team. Nowadays the posters all around town say, "Run, Ryan, Run!" but when he began, the sight of a teen pounding out miles was unusual enough that some lowered their car windows to holler, "Run, Forrest, run!" When Hall and his parents relate these stories, amusement trumps animus. "There just weren't funds for a track team," says Mickey. "Besides, he was getting to do everything we wanted him to do without being on a team." Now, thanks to Ryan's high profile and the efforts of a local reporter who raced for Mickey in high school, Big Bear Lake has both track and cross-country teams, and Ryan has lent his support to the Lighthouse Project—a local organization dedicated to creating "child-honoring communities." Farther afield, Ryan and Sara are members of Team World Vision, a charity designed to promote self-sustaining communities in Africa. The couple speak eagerly of the time when they will be able to serve as missionaries in Africa.

As Hall eats chicken salad with a plastic fork, fellow church members stop by to say hello. They call him "Ry," and happily tell visitors stories about the little boy they knew. The fellow across the table couldn't give two hoots about Beijing and keeps steering the conversation back to trout fishing and his half-wolf dog.

The utter lack of obsequiousness is a reminder that the Lord need not rain down disappointing splits and shinsplints to keep his servants humble. His touch can be ineffably deft. A man who has been studying Hall from a distance leans to his wife's ear and asks a question. "Yes!" she says, brightly. "He's going to the Olympics!" He leans to her ear again. "No, no," she says, still beaming. "In *cross-country!*"

You can ask a man questions. You can observe him about his daily business. You can even sit beside him in church. But in your heart you know it's presumptive to think your brief window can illuminate his soul. It is likewise tempting to posit a natural connection between spirituality and long-distance running. Even at the basest amateur level, running is predicated on periods of extended isolation, meditative rhythm, and regular access to the deoxygenated edge of failure (where the best revelations reside). Hall has been quoted saying that he saw the scarred body of Christ during the last two miles of the 2007 London Marathon. And yet, one shouldn't get carried away. When he speaks of his faith in his laid-back California accent, it's unlikely he'll knock you off your seat. Hall is neither fiery nor overly eloquent in defense of his faith. Remember his words to describe the moment God spoke to him at Big Bear Lake? *I describe it as a vision, but you could call it an idea, whatever* . . . Disarming but not disarmed, he acknowledges skepticism even as he remains resolute in faith.

"It's not my goal to convert anyone, you know," he says in a conversation at the Olympic Training Center in Chula Vista. "I think Jesus *invited* people to hear what he had to say. I think he told people what was in his heart. I want to be authentic with people . . . for me not to share why I run or what gets me through hard moments in races would be cheating them. But I'm not going to force someone to hear something they're not interested in hearing." *Do the work, Ryan. Leave the rest to God.* Over and over his father has told him this, but he would dearly love to win in Beijing. He is not impervious. After losing to Alan Webb in the mile at the 2001 Arcadia Invitational, he flung his shoes and went for a long run barefoot. After the Pac-10 Cross-Country Championships in Arizona, Mickey and Susie found him weeping in the bushes. Last year, prior to the Trials, he told his mother he had promised God he would have a better attitude whenever he didn't do well. "I told him, 'Expect to be tested on that,'" says Susie Hall, eyes twinkling. "And then he had three bad races leading up to the Trials. He needed to be humbled. People relate far more to the disappointment than the celebration." (True enough, but oh, that finish at the Trials.)

The day before we attended church in Big Bear Lake, I accompanied Hall on a pair of recovery runs at the Olympic Training Center. To keep things fair, I rode a bicycle lent to me by 5,000-meter specialist Ian Dobson. Terrified I would veer in too close and be forever known as the man who ruptured the Achilles of the most promising US marathoner in two decades, I followed at a safe distance, which is to say I watched Hall run from a perspective shared by 99 percent of his recent competitors. I was struck by the immaculate nature of his footfalls. Each heel came to earth perfectly square, with no hint of pronation. "His stride was gorgeous from the beginning," says Mickey Hall. "His legs would just flow." His torso, on the other hand, is held parsimoniously erect as if to provide the heart and lungs a stable work environment. The stiffness continues in the specific alignment of his thumbs, pointed forward from atop his fists. His elbows are held at right angles and sweep back and forth just above the iliac crest, crossing at the same plane every time. His left elbow wings out a tad—a teensy imperfection held over from an early habit of crossing his body with his arms. Mickey spotted this early and mostly cured it by tying Ryan's elbow to his side.

But Mickey is right: Everything is extraneous to those legs. You can see them in footage from the homestretch of the Trials, turning over in a pinwheeling lope, each foot meeting the earth right on axis, then looping up and away to fly forward again. The legs are all business right to the finish, even as the arms begin to loosen, even as Hall's head begins to swivel to acknowledge the noise of the crowd. The closer he draws to the line, the more evident it is that this is a finish for the ages. Hall begins to gesticulate, pointing to the sky, raising his arms high, even slapping hands with the people crowding the course. At first it seems uncharacteristic based on what you know of Hall and his mellow Christian demeanor. Then you notice the blazing intensity of his eyes and the inclusiveness of his open arms, and you realize he is not exulting, but exhorting. He is not celebrating triumph over man but rather triumph in the Lord—in short, this is a man in rapture. Hall often refers to running in terms of sanctuary, and here he is now, Brother Lawrence in a singlet, twining work to worship, running 4:55 splits, praising God full tilt right until he breaks across the line and the only thing left to do is bow quietly down, the work all done, the victory won.

It has been a long day for the Hall family. After the church luncheon, the television crew and I return to their house for a final round of interviews. Susie spreads photo albums on the kitchen table (should you ever qualify for the Olympics, know that the picture of you wearing an Olympics sweatshirt, a diaper, and your sister's tap shoes will wind up on TV) and serves fresh-baked apple muffins as she runs around the house gathering mementos from Ryan's career. She has to dig around some. "We don't keep a shrine to Ryan," says Susie. "We have five children. We could fill the walls with his things, but we try to celebrate the gifts each of them have." Ryan and Mickey sit down together and talk for the cameras some, then do a father-son run for yet more B-roll. Finally Ryan—who has learned the lesson of rest and follows a strict regimen of icing, recovery, and massage—leaves for an appointment with his masseuse.

So now the final piece of gear is packed as sunlight slides through the pine trees at a flattening slant. In the living room, Mickey Hall cues up footage of Ryan's triumphant finish in the Trials. Susie and Ryan's grandmother Madeline join them, and for a while everyone just watches, eyes raised to the screen. Eventually, Susie speaks. "You know, for three days before every one of Ryan's races, Mickey fasts and prays. He prays that it will be a good race and a safe race." Up on the screen Ryan is surging for the finish, strong as a bolting deer, glorifying the Lord with each step. You think of Mickey, on his knees and hungry (so weak one time he fell and wound up in the ER), beseeching that same Lord that He might deliver every runner safe to the finish line. And yet we know full well watching the footage now, that even as Ryan Hall was pointing to the sky and the crowd was making a *crazy* joyful noise, his friend Ryan Shay was dead. The following night Mickey dined with Shay's father-in-law. "What do you say to someone who's lost their son?" he says, shaking his head. "What do you say?" The questions are not new, and hang in the air. God's mystery will be revealed, answer the believers; grim coincidence, say the nonbelievers.

Hall has at times gone out of his way to play down attempts by outsiders to overpersonalize the tragedy by casting him and Shay as best friends, but in the month following the Trials, he and Sara quietly moved in with Alicia in Flagstaff, and Hall will tell you that he trains for the Olympics with Shay's memory a constant companion. It would be easy to nudge the narrative toward that end. To set the possibility of Ryan Hall ascending the center dais as Ryan Shay's spirit made visible. It could happen, and Hall will be thrilled if he runs to victory. But he knows first and foremost he must run to honor the Lord.

Ryan Hall's grandmother is suddenly at my elbow. Her face is troubled. All day she has been a sparkling presence. A petite woman with glittering eyes, she is lovingly teased by her family for her vociferous cheering at Ryan's races. In private company she is quick to laugh and often punctuates her asides with a knowing grin. But now the house is quiet—Mickey has his son paused up there on the screen—and the glitter in her eyes has gone wet.

"I want you to know . . ." says Madeline, faltering. "I want you to know that this family prays, and prays for many things. That it will be a good race, that it will be a safe race, but they never . . . they never . . ." She stops now, holding her hand to her mouth as her eyes fill with tears. It takes her a moment to gather before she can speak again.

"They *never* pray to win."

2008

P.S. Hall finished 10th in Beijing. In 2011 he placed fourth in the Boston Marathon, running the fastest marathon ever by an American. He retired in 2016.

P.P.S. Does anyone remember the Bobbsey Twins?

RUNNING THE RIVER RIGHTEOUS

Steve Austin believes the Earth is 10,000 years old, and he has led us to the rock that proves it. We are in the Grand Canyon, standing on a slope of tumbled boulders above the Colorado River, just downstream from the inlet of the Little Colorado. We arrived on a pair of giant blue rafts now tethered in the aquamarine water below. Austin's right arm is extended, his hand arranged in a hang-loose configuration, middle fingers curled, pinkie and thumb framing a gap between two rock strata. Geologists refer to this gap as the Great Unconformity, because it represents a set of missing levels in the giant layer cake that is the Grand Canyon. Most scientists think those layers were scrubbed away during a period of gentle erosion lasting millions of years. Austin says such talk is hogwash. As a Young-Earth Creation scientist, he believes God created Heaven and Earth in six literal, nonallegorical, 24-hour solar days. He theorizes that the missing strata were blasted away in just days by the onset of Noah's flood, after which the gathering and receding waters deposited 4,000 feet of new rock above—all in a bit more than a year. Resting his hand on the formation below the gap, Austin lectures, "This was preflood ocean floor, formed a little after day three of creation. This is the closest we get to the Earth that Noah walked on."

A cluster of believers stand among the boulders below him, listening intently. Several will clamber up to touch the rock before we depart. Raising his hand to take the measure of the gap again, Austin, who has a PhD in geology from Penn State, dismisses the idea that millions of years passed between the erosion and deposition of the two layers. "We marvel at the absence of the evidence," he says. "Creationists are pointing to what we see; evolutionists point to what we don't see." It is a statement that begs parsing. It is a statement that convolutes the very concept of faith.

My faith is currently adrift somewhere in the straits of befuddled existential agnosticism. I said as much to the woman from the Institute for Creation Research (ICR) when I called to reserve a spot on a nine-day canyon tour featuring Christ-centered rafting. As it developed, she was more concerned about my being a writer than a sinner, but we worked that out. "I think you'll meet some very nice people," she said.

I didn't doubt it. I was raised a fundamentalist Christian, and while I no longer believe, it is not a scorched-earth situation. For the most part, the Christians I worshipped with were a humble, tolerant bunch, content to choose example over harangue. As do most strays, however, I carry a little residual crankiness. The *What Would Jesus Do?* thing sets my teeth on edge as a peppy pop-culture gloss on the sweaty spiritual wrassling that troubled souls endure. And when one of my fellow rafters approached me prior to launch and asked if I was a Christian, I got my back up a little, asking him if he would treat me differently depending on my answer.

But these trivial grumbles did little to diminish my growing excitement for the trip. Christ-centered or not, I was hungry for my first taste of whitewater. Once, many years ago, I hiked in and out of the Canyon, and I remember gazing down, longing to run the blue-green thread below. Over the next week we would follow that thread from Lee's Ferry, 15 miles south of the Glen Canyon Dam, a winding 88 miles to the depths of the gorge at the foot of the Bright Angel Trail. I was eager to run the rapids and eager to let the canyon roil the vestiges of my own latent faith. I was also struck with how "baptize" rhymes with "capsize."

◆ ◆ ◆

We launch on a Monday morning. A small flotilla of rafts is moored along the beach at Lee's Ferry, each served by its own roped-off loading lane. Guides from the various services rib and hail each other knowingly while we greenhorns mill dumbly. Mostly you hear the sounds of preparation: the scuff of a duffel being dragged over gravel, the plasticky clink of a life preserver buckle, the squinch of a sandal sole skidding on a rubber raft tube. Several of the adjacent craft are taking on crates of beer. Our crew is mixing coolers of Crystal Light.

Lead boatman Tom Vail provides our safety orientation. Beginning with a well-worn but funny line ("Rafting is safer than golf, but more dangerous than bowling"), he addresses us from the prow of the raft, reviewing elements of safety and comportment, drawing our attention to pinch points on the hinged deck, demonstrating proper safety strap use, reviewing the rules on standing and sitting, even providing peeing instructions. Someone inquires about dinner, but Vail cuts him off. "I'll cover that before we make camp." He's quick to grin, but he frequently adopts the persona of a drill sergeant in flip-flops.

Vail has been running the river for 21 years. He is full-bearded and stocky. You look at him and think, *hearty.* Back in the 1980s, Vail traded a corporate gig in Los Angeles for the back end of a raft, and he's been here ever since. He has recently attracted national attention for his book *Grand Canyon: A Different View,* in which he details his conversion from beer-drinking river-ripper to creationist acolyte. When the coffee-table book, supplemented with essays by theologians and like-minded scientists, was made available for sale in National Park Service bookstores, geologists and common citizens alike protested what they maintained was government-sanctioned promulgation of religious beliefs posing as geologic theory. Vail has weathered the criticism resolutely, if a bit peevishly, but today he is visibly buoyed by the prospect of sharing the river with like-minded believers.

In the church of my youth, the women wore modest dresses and always kept their hair up in buns. While women were forbidden to cut their hair, long hair on a man was an abomination. Television and dancing were not allowed. My parents stood firm on these tenets, but they were also kind and loving. It would be overdramatic for me to claim I suffered any undue hardship under the proscriptions of our faith. Nonetheless, I felt out of place among worldly people. Once a year, our congregation withdrew to a rural farmstead for four days of worship. These were times of deep comfort. It was a delight to mingle with people of one accord. When we raised our voices to sing or lowered our heads to pray, there was no one to sneer or snicker. So I understand the joy of fellowship. I know how Tom Vail feels back there on the tiller as we pull away from the beach and push into the current. His soul is wide open and his heart is full as he captains a boatload of faithful believers down the center aisle of what he calls God's gargantuan cathedral.

In 1994, Steve Austin coauthored a book of his own: *Grand Canyon: Monument to Catastrophe.* In the preface, Austin says Christians compromise their faith if they visit the Grand Canyon and accept the prevalent evolutionary interpretation of its formation. Throughout the trip Austin urges rafters to compose "talking points" so that they are prepared to spread the gospel of creationism upon their return to the rim world.

Counting the four boatmen, there are 34 of us arranged on the two blue 37-foot rafts. As near as I can determine, only three of us—me, and the two guys piloting the second raft—are non-believers. Our group includes a doctor, a pathologist, a chiropractor and his grandson, a mother and her young daughter, a homeschooling family of four, a former firefighter, a creation scientist from England, and a pair of retired chicken farmers. Several of the group are wearing T-shirts embossed with a graphic depicting the Grand Canyon strata. The rafts are barely under way when Austin points to the Kaibab Limestone rising beside us and says, "We're at the top of the T-shirt!" In the coming days, we'll trace the strata on our chests one colored bar at a time as we descend through riffle and rapid, deeper and deeper into this great cleft worn—one way or another—into the Earth.

Here's how most scientists see it. The Kaibab Limestone, the most common cap rock in the area, is thought to be 260 million years old, while the gneiss and schist exposed at the base of the canyon are pegged somewhere around 1.8 billion years. Widely accepted geologic theory states that the Earth we see today exists as the result of forces having acted uniformly from the origin of the planet to the present—a school of thought described broadly as uniformitarianism. That would mean the Grand Canyon is roughly five to six million years old (though the initial carving may have commenced 70 million years ago). Most geologists believe it was sculpted by the forces of erosion and abrasion, and that the lower 2,000 feet of the canyon—almost half its depth—may have been carved in the last 750,000 years. In the world of uniformitarian geology and mainstream science, 750,000 years is an instant.

Yet for Young-Earth Creationists, the canyon was formed in a real-life geologic instant. They do not believe this place was borne out of gentle scrubbing; they think it was power-washed in the wake of, to quote ICR president emeritus Henry Morris, "[God's] world-convulsing judgment." To spread their geologic gospel, ICR uses newsletters, books, DVDs, radio shows, public lectures, and even their own museum and graduate school (where Austin serves as professor of geology), but none of these can convey the message with the power of the Grand Canyon. With its exposed landforms, strata, and fossils, it is the ur-classroom. In the spirit of Martin Luther, creationists come here to tack their own thesis on the door of orthodoxy.

• • •

You do not actually enter the Grand Canyon until you've passed the confluence of the Little Colorado 61 miles downstream from Lee's Ferry; until then you're in Marble Canyon. But the feeling that you've entered another world is immediate. The walls shoot up, and even though you know they'll rise thousands of feet farther still, thoughts of cosmic relativity are insinuating themselves by mile three. A white-throated swift, gnatlike in the upper reaches, flutters above the rim and banks away, sunlight flaring along the trailing edge of its fixed wings. A bighorn sheep rests in the tamarisk, motionless but for the pulse of its flank. A lizard on a hot rock warns us away with a chesty set of pushups, unmindful of the conflict in the Middle East, the possibility of life on Mars, or the overwhelming force inherent in a size 10 boot. In this respect, he proves to be no more solipsistic or ludicrous than we are.

Austin is standing toward the rear of the raft, and he lectures as we float. His voice is resolutely professorial but it imparts a compressed excitement. Beneath the flat, scholarly affect he conveys a great eagerness to share belief. When we pull into an alcove to view the petroglyph of a geologist's rock hammer left by a USGS crew in 1923, he points to features carved into the surrounding rock by erosive forces. "Uniformitarians limit these forces to solution [a chemical process in which rocks are dissolved by a liquid] and abrasion," he says. "I add plucking and cavitation." Plucking involves water slamming against rock at a velocity sufficient to dislodge blocks of material; cavitation occurs when fluids flowing at high velocity form vacuum bubbles that implode. If you think of solution and abrasion as fine sandpaper, then plucking and cavitation would be geologic jackhammers. If you're going to advance the theory of a fast-tracked canyon, you can acknowledge the sandpaper, but you *need* the jackhammers—the combination is familiar to any mainstream geologist, but Austin dubs it "Austin's four means of erosion."

As the professor expounds, the rafters murmur and take pictures. A passenger in sunglasses and a cowboy hat bends his head over a small notebook. He will write steadily throughout the trip and will sit atop his bedroll in the evenings, studying his notes. He says he's eager to share what he learns with church groups back home.

The day slides by beautifully. We drift past clots of moss and lone trout. We were tentative and polite at launch, but the first walloping dollop of ice water dissolved all social reserve, leaving us dripping with giddy chatter. Sometimes the rapids break over the prow with such force that I am lifted from my seat and washed backward, kept aboard only by my death grip on the safety straps. At one point I feel sure I have swimmer's boogers, but I'm having so much fun I don't care.

We roast in the sun between rapids, and the float is a lark. But by early afternoon we are in shadow, and I am quickly shivering. Cold diuresis compounds my discomfort, forcing fluid from my constricted surface blood vessels through my kidneys and into my bladder. I am shortly in dire need of a pee. I sit rock still, as the slightest movement triggers stabbing cramps. We seem to float forever. When our raft bumps the shore, I commit the grave error of allowing myself to believe relief is nigh only to hear Tom Vail bellow, "Stay on the boats!"

Up until now I have been outwardly stoic, but at this command, I let slip a little moan. People began milling the second the rafts touched sand, and Vail has yet to cover the rules of camp. He reverts to herding mode, aware that once he turns us loose we'll scatter like first graders at recess. He describes the unloading procedure, and I am listening, but I am hunched like a beat dog, desperate to keep the pressure off my bladder. By the time he tells us where to stake out our sleeping areas, I am certain I am doing myself damage. I am determined to be a decent, well-behaved boater, but when he begins reviewing toilet protocol, I bail over the edge of the raft and let go.

Vail prefers this campsite because its relatively compact layout keeps everyone together to learn the camp routine and get better acquainted. We set up a fire line and unpack the rafts in short order. I am wearing dry socks and underwear—certainly one of the top 10 ineffable comforts available to man. After a dinner of salmon steaks, the group convenes for a brief devotional, and when darkness descends, we take to bed. I am lying with my head to the wall and my feet to the river. The man bunking adjacent to me is a physician from the Midwest. We discuss meth labs and renegade Amish youth, and through chance conversation, discover there are two degrees of separation between us and a recently deceased bike mechanic in Carbondale, Illinois. "Hey," he says, "there's the Big Dipper!" Sure enough, there it is, ladling over backward above us. Across the river, the towering rock face is a black bulk, and then, about three-quarters of the way up, its face breaks sharply white, soaked in moonrise. The delineation of the horizon is so exact, the projected light so electric, it is as if a ghostly locomotive hovers at the rim above, pushing nearer and nearer. The feeling is that something big impends. So, I guess, it has ever been.

In no time, the river days take on a rhythm. I wake each morning to the concussive *whump* of fiberglass supply lids dropping shut on the amidships food compartments. Shortly thereafter comes the holler, "Coffeee's readyyy!" and the day begins. After breakfast and more devotions, we load the rafts and hit the river, making occasional stops for side trips. Austin narrates the emerging strata nonstop, rarely taking his seat, pointing to this or that formation and correlating it to geology and scripture.

At mile 33, we stop to explore Redwall Cavern. Austin leads us past a group of secular rafters playing Wiffle ball to a rock containing tiny fossils. Austin identifies a white fossil shaped roughly like a golf tee. "Crinoids are marine animals known to deteriorate shortly after death," says Austin. "This one has maintained its original shape and is fossilized intact, indicating that it was buried rapidly."

A little farther downriver, he guides us to an exposed section of Redwall limestone studded with nautiloid fossils. Nautiloids were large squidlike creatures possessing conical multichambered shells. They have roughly the same dimensions as an overgrown zucchini. In his research Austin once plotted the orientation of a dozen Redwall nautiloids to show that 10 of them were aligned in one plane, evidence to him that the creatures were under the influence of a strong current when they were encased in sediment. As we study the fossils ourselves, Austin points out shattered shells and says the chambers imploded under intense compression. "If you were standing here when this burial occurred," he says, "it would be very much like an underwater avalanche."

Austin is especially pleased to remind us that nautiloids of various sizes are found throughout the Redwall, saying this demonstrates that we're viewing remnants of a nearly instantaneous mass kill. Austin claims mainstream scientists were amazed that he found the fossils in such conglomeration, and he maintains their incredulity was due in part to the fact that they were not thinking in catastrophic terms. "This is an extraordinary event, requiring an extraordinary explanation," he says. Then he grins, and adds, "I guess you find what you're looking for."

The rafters scramble around the Redwall shelves, ranging out to locate their own nautiloids, finger painting them with water so they take on color and show up in snapshots. The chiropractor says touching the fossils bolsters his faith. "If I can believe the Earth things I see, then it helps me to believe the other things about God that I can't see." I touch one myself, and get a little spooky in the gut thinking about the world that once was. So many mysteries and no one to ask, and so we rely on the interpretations of man. Later, surrounded by an audience of rafters and a two-man film crew hired by ICR to document the trip, Austin repeats his nautiloid lecture. When he finishes, the group applauds. I recall something Austin said the day we met: "What we're talking about today may become accepted doctrine in the textbooks 25 years from now." Later that night, we make fajitas and sing hymns beneath the open sky. I am warmed by the combination of bonhomie and solemnity, but I can't help wondering where I would stand if one of these nice people petitioned the school board to incorporate their film into the science curriculum at my local high school.

The day before we descended into the canyon, we attended church services on the rim. After hymns and prayer, a preacher from ICR got to going, and brother, he could bring it. I like some good preaching, and this was that. He paced the riser, he found his cadence, and he worked it. He took it up, and he took it down. He spoke of invisible things, of how man can define God only in the things He has made, which means we have all seen God, which means we are left no excuse for disbelief. He got some *mm-hmms* with that one. Riffing in the area of Romans 1:22, he spoke of men so full of their own philosophy they become blind to what God has made. He mentioned Carl Sagan, and did a little *billions and billions* impression. Then the preacher came to a full stop, stage right, and looked out at us with his head at an impish tilt. Stood there silent for two beats, then said, "By the way, Carl knows what's goin' on *now!*" The congregation bubbled with chuckles. The preacher held the smug pose, one hand tucked aw-shucks style in his pants pocket, the other held flat beneath the splayed Bible from which he had been quoting without looking. As the chuckles spread, the preacher rolled his eyes and gave that Bible a little bounce. And I'll tell you, he lost me right there. You want to lure me back, brother, show some compassion. Before honor is humility, if you'll allow me a little Old Testament. Drop to your knees and pray through tears that our fellow sinner Carl might yet be redeemed. What you had here was a little jig danced on a lost soul. I had heard those chuckles before, from people of my own congregation, as they listened to one of our preachers tell how he turned his back on a struggling member after he caught her wearing shorts. From that day forward, I've tried to reconcile the deep goodness of my childhood church with its poisonous little seams of petty certitude. I found myself doing a similar thing in the canyon, trying to reconcile the chuckles on the rim with the sincere smiles all around me.

The thing is, as we float deeper and deeper into the canyon and creationism, I want to believe, if only to please these people. Rafting with this group is a joy. No one cusses or gets drunked up. Women are treated with respect. A sunny collegiality prevails. There is never a shortage of folks to lug gear or set up the kitchen or slice the peppers. Based on a survey of heathen boatmen, it seems you can set up camp a heck of a lot more efficiently with a boatload of Promise Keepers than you can with blissed-out Earth worshippers or sunburned party animals. I credit the Crystal Light.

Perhaps it is my eagerness to please, and perhaps it is some variation on Stockholm syndrome, but I find myself leaning Steve Austin's way. Caught in this vacuum, his observations make sense. At the very least, I am coming to believe that his research is worthy if only for forcing a reexamination of established paradigms. While I'm not buying the Young-Earth theory, I'm intrigued by the role catastrophic forces may have played in forming the canyon. On day three, we hike to a giant fold in the otherwise horizontally oriented layers of Tapeats sandstone. Austin explains that in order for a rock to fold, it must have been softened by floodwaters (after all, molten rock would have metamorphosed and the stratifications disappeared). The fold is right there before me, big as a barn, hard as a rock. I squint against the beating sun and hear a niggling voice: *what if he's right?*

I join the group for morning and evening devotionals whenever possible. I enjoy the hymns. I always have. The singing is simple and strong like it was when I was still going to church, the women harmonizing high and plain, the men holding notes risen from chests built to stand the storm. A good hymn-sing makes you believe in the possibility of wings. Tom Vail gave his testimony last night, and when he spoke of his conversion, his voice broke with tears. I know that moment. As a young boy I answered the preacher's call in the basement of the Moose Hall, rising to my feet to profess my faith before God and man. Your face contorts with repentance and relief, and the tears break loose. When the rafters bowed their heads to pray, I bowed my own, grateful for this moment of peace at the end of the day, grateful for the steady presence of the river.

While it's fun to adopt a seasoned gaze and tell folks you've been whitewater rafting, the truth is, running rapids in a big blue raft is like hitting potholes in a Hummer. You understand that it's rough out there, but the vehicle absorbs the worst of it. Trey, our boatman, remains laid-back and sunglassed at the tiller even as we rock and whoop through the tumult, but if you listen, you can hear little bursts of gunning back there as he fires the outboard, a hint that he's tweaking our trajectory on the fly. After guiding us through several rapids so dexterously we barely moisten our scuba boots, he asks, "You guys wanna get wet?" Everyone grins, and on our next run, he plunges the nose through a wall of water. The raft shudders heavily and then churns through. Trey kills the motor, and we are back to sightseeing.

There are black stains all along the canyon wall. I am wearing polarized sunglasses, and if I twist my head, the stains flash alternately silver and black. I ask Austin about this, and he says I am seeing rock varnish, formed when airborne particles cling to wet stone. "It is crystalline in nature," says Austin, "thus the polarized iridescence." There is a slight pause, then he adds, "And, it's an accreted feature, disproving the theory that time wears the canyon down."

That last observation feels tacked on, but Austin is a hard man to read. He operates with a sort of studied distraction. He has a habit of launching sentences with a prefatory "Okay," and he repeats the phrase as he narrates, whether discussing Zoroaster granite or the trials of Job. It's the habit of a man used to explaining things. When he gets rolling, a touch of hubris can creep in. Answering a question about a geological dispute involving features of the Redwall limestone, he brags, "There is no intertonguing. I trashed that. So that's my contribution to the Redwall. That, and the nautiloid bed."

We anchor at the Unkar Delta, and a boatman leads us to an Anasazi ruin, where he gives a detailed history of the people. This thoroughly lapsed stepson-of-a-Baptist preacher knows his Bible and has been quietly fuming throughout the trip, gawking openly at some of Austin's claims. "We can learn much from what the Anasazi left behind," the boatman says. "For instance, from the fact that some of their pottery shards are decorated, we can extrapolate that they had leisure time." That triggers a skeptical interjection from Tom Vail: "When you hear about the leaps these archaeologists make, you have to ask yourself: does this make sense?" Four miles downriver, we beach the rafts again and hike up 75 Mile Creek to view the Shinumo quartzite. Austin traces its wildly swirled appearance to Genesis 1:9, when God separated water from land. "It was the most stupendous tectonic event on Earth," he says. "This was unstable, water-saturated sand. Then it got hit with the earthquake, swirled, and hardened, leaving the characteristic ripple effect." He pats the rock. "This is day three of creation you're looking at." I think about what Tom Vail said just four miles back. I am getting to the point where I want to look at a rock and see just a rock.

Creation scientists are caught in a fundamental conundrum. They're using the tools and measures of man to disprove the tools and measures of man. One of ICR's research initiatives is the so-called RATE Project, in which they're attempting to prove that radioisotope dating techniques that put the age of the Earth in the billions of years are wholly inaccurate. Should their scientists fail to achieve the proper results, ICR will undoubtedly search for new ways to prove that the Earth is young. In the end, using scientific literalism to support theological literalism is likely to beget trouble.

I do not believe, but I am not scoffing. (Tell the preacher with the bouncy Bible that I have read 2 Peter 3:3.) There's enough derision in the world. Nonetheless, as we draw near the end of our river trip, I have grown weary of the nonstop determination to jam every nook and cranny of this place into conformity with God's plan as interpreted by man. Just across the Colorado from the Great Unconformity—that seminal Creationist touchstone—you will find salt seeps holy to the Hopi. We have been projecting our various spiritualities on this place since the first set of human eyes beheld it. Draw a great gash in the Earth and it will fill with pilgrims. Everybody wants to claim nature for themselves, for God, or as God. In fairness, I indict myself, as well as the gung-ho *What Would Kokopelli Do?* crowd (whom ye shall know by their bike racks). The spiritualization of everything necessitates a trivialization that ultimately weakens the construct. During our bus ride out of Phoenix, someone offered a prayer for the driver, and I wondered if we might not also pray for the guy who tightened the lug nuts or adjusted the brakes. Before the launch, God was very specifically asked to prevent twisted ankles. When one of the group twisted his ankle, it begged the question: Was this the will of God, and if it was, was the request misguided in the first place? Once you start with this stuff, it never ends. If you come to this cleft in the globe to sort out all of creation, you quickly find there are enough puzzle pieces out here to last an eternity. From river bend to river bend, you look up and see the Grand Canyon is constantly reframing the world.

Our final day on the river, we took one last side trip, hiking up into Clear Creek Canyon. The waterfall there splits in two. One half pours straight down over your head. The other careens off the rocks to hit you from the side. Everyone takes turns in the water, and it's a joyful scene. The rocks echo with hoots and hollers. The chicken farmers, nimble and spry after 47 years of marriage ("dating for 51 and a half," confides the wife with a grin), hold hands in the spray. The homeschoolers pose for a family picture. Steve Austin frolics with his young son, just a dad with his boy. In the moment they aren't fundamentalists or dogmatists or creationists—they're shiny happy people. To a person, they've been decent and considerate of me. One more time, I wish I could please them by believing.

That night, Tom Vail fires me as we're prepping dinner. Having been promoted to assistant griddle minder on the basis of my knife-handling skills, I'm summarily busted to dishwasher after failing to properly solve the equations required to make six boxes of stuffing in a steel pail. Vail delivers the bad news with a grin and a belly laugh. My favorite sort of person is a sinner with a work ethic, but a fundamentalist Christian with a sense of humor covers a lot of ground.

In light of my experience, it troubles me to think in adversarial terms, but there will be a battle. It is already being fought. More and more creationists are taking their cause to the schools. In Cobb County, Georgia, for instance, the local school district is embroiled in legal battles after posting disclaimers in science textbooks stating that "evolution is a theory, not a fact." In a speech welcoming us on the trip, ICR president John Morris said, "The flood is the key. You gotta get the flood right. When we get the flood right, we *win*." It will be messy. Books, magazines, journal articles, and online resources proliferate on both sides. As in politics, opposing forces are represented by experts fluent in blizzards of counter-minutiae. The theories of Steve Austin have been sliced six ways to Sunday by the traditional science community. If the canyon was cut immediately after the flood, how did the mile-high water-saturated walls remain standing? A raging river should cut a straight line, not a meandering line. The fold in the Tapeats sandstone is the result of plastic changes over millions of years. Dead nautiloids may indicate a mass kill, but the absence of other fossils questions the viability of a worldwide flood theory. What about dinosaur fossils embedded in the rock supposedly deposited after the flood? And what about all the scientific consensus behind radioisotope dating?

Trouble is, presenting counterarguments is like trying to study a raindrop in a hurricane. Refutation begets counter-refutation. Andrew Snelling, the other ICR geologist on the trip, asked if I'd heard the joke about the 15 geologists who stood on a rock outcropping and offered 16 theories as to how it was formed. A thinking layperson is reduced to reading the polemics and broadsides and drawing conclusions based on faith, evidence, or both. At this point in my search for understanding, I believe the earth is very, very old. But ultimately, I do not care how it all came to be. The comment is neither flip nor snotty. From the depths of my soul, should I prove to have one, I do not care. The same people who say God has revealed himself to all men overlook the fact that He may have told the rest of us something different. The journey of faith is constant—there is grave danger in assuming you have arrived. The Grand Canyon makes me feel humble. That will do for now.

I exchanged e-mails with a few of the rafters after our trip. They were united in their belief that the trip had bolstered their belief. "Some people confuse objectivity and truth," wrote the pathologist. "God and His word are truth . . . calls for objectivity usually mean consider other ideas—usually of man's thought." "For those who disagree with us," wrote another rafter, "they are welcome to say we are not objective or even to call us fools."

I am thinking of this kind of resolve on our third night out, just at dusk. I am unpacking my gear in a rocky penthouse overlooking the campsite when I realize I have missed the beginning of the evening devotional. I unroll my sleeping bag, kill the flashlight, and watch from above. I catch bits and pieces. Steve is speaking on Genesis, chapter 7. The part about the fountains of the great deep. Next I hear the murmur of prayer. And then, a final hymn. It floats up to the rocks as a soft drone. I find it a comfort. It is fully dark now, and as the last note of worship fades, a miniature galaxy of 30-some headlamps and flashlights switch on. They cluster for a bit, weaving in and among each other, then begin to strike out, dispersing along the beach and through the invisible tamarisk, each little light cutting its own true course through the darkness all around us.

2004

P.S. I hiked all the way out of the canyon and was in my hotel room when I discovered a big rock in the bottom of my backpack. It occurred to me that one of the boatmen, known as a prankster, had a particular twinkle in his eye as he bid me good-bye.

SUBLIMATION: THE BLIND BOYS OF ALABAMA

One day my neighbor called. He was recording an album.
Wondered if I'd write the liner notes. The studio was just a
couple cornfields away, so I drove over there.

All around, the world was white. The snow that winter had fallen
in Biblical proportions. Into this clean-slate landscape stepped
four blind men from Alabama. They came to sing the Gospel.

Waiting were two Midwestern men. Justin Vernon and Phil
Cook were boys in a band when they discovered the music of Sam
Cooke. Then they discovered Sam Cooke songs about Jesus. But
these were not *hymns*. Hereabouts, hymns were measured and
staid. In Cooke's music the boys heard the lexicon of faith, but
the rhythm—the soul—of something else entirely. From Cooke
they moved to the Staple Singers . . . Sister Rosetta Tharpe . . .
Mahalia Jackson . . . and one day they discovered the Blind Boys
of Alabama.

In time the two men grew up and drew apart. There were
wounds in that, although even now they would agree their accumulated hours of darkness had been at worst slightly cloudy.
But when the shadows fell, each man turned to the holy blues.
And among the most consoling lights that shone on them were
the Blind Boys of Alabama. And now these men of the south were
finding their way north, passing between bare trees to a snow-
bound building off a Wisconsin country road.

◆ ◆ ◆

The room built to capture sound was cut squarely into the northern soil, solidly sunk below the frost line, embanked in earthen stillness. Upstairs the men stomped their boots clean and prepared to descend. Downstairs, the music—in the form of air yet to be breathed—waited.

◆ ◆ ◆

When sustaining legends cross your threshold, you show respect and deference. And then you get to work. The session lasted four days. In the studio, and at the table over bread broken between takes, there were those who believed and those who wondered. But the great miraculous mystery of gospel music lies less in its power over believers and more in its power to move those who believe otherwise, or those who believe not at all. Thus Dr. King addressed a split nation in cadence drawn from pulpit and song. When there is glory in the throat, every listener dares dream of grand transcendence.

One night as the recording went on, there was a knock at the door. Neighbors from up the road. A young girl and her father, the girl on the cusp of her teens. She knew nothing of the Alabamans. She stood in the shadow of a corner and listened. *Please,* sang the man at the microphone, *please take me to the water,* and on the way home, in the dark as snow squeaked beneath the wheels, the girl said, *I will remember this night for all my life.*

◆ ◆ ◆

There is a point at the dead center of winter when it is difficult to summon the memory of green. Every branch is black against the sky, and leaves exist only as an article of faith. Imagine then, a photograph of a sweet green tree. The tree is on an island, alone. The encircling water appears white. So white it could be snow. The whiteness leaves the tree skirted in mystery. Rooted in this world, and yet otherworldly. The tree says heaven is nearer than we know. That heaven is recognizable. That there are things to be seen even if we cannot see.

• • •

If you were raised in snow, you know of its pure miracle: On the clearest, coldest days, the crystals pass to vapor with no pause to be liquid. *Sublimation.* From the Latin, meaning "raised up." When the last song was sung, there were drifts to the door. The four blind men formed a line, each man's hand on the shoulder of the man before him, and stepped surefootedly into the white.

ACKNOWLEDGMENTS

My parents—anything decent is because of them, anything else is simply not their fault.

My wife and daughters. For all my absences, our dinner table time is all the more dear.

Lisa Bankoff (with her cast and crew), my guide and champion.

Alissa Freeberg, professional minder and reminder.

Blakeley Beatty, booking the book guy.

Kate, Kathy, Kristin, Halley, Emily, and Elizabeth at the Wisconsin Historical Society Press.

And, one more time as coda to the Introduction: the multitude of editors and fact-checkers whose diligence, patience, and exhortations were—and are—ever essential. Thank you for guiding and correcting me in my work.

ABOUT THE AUTHOR

Michael Perry is the *New York Times* bestselling author of numerous books, including *Population: 485* (recently adapted for the stage), *Truck: A Love Story,* and *The Jesus Cow.* His live humor recordings include *Never Stand Behind a Sneezing Cow* and *The Clodhopper Monologues,* and he is currently recording a third album of music with his band, the Long Beds. He lives in rural Wisconsin with his wife and daughters and is privileged to serve as a first responder with the local fire department. He can be found online at www.sneezingcow.com.